THUNDERHEAD RISING ABOVE MOUNDS OF ANCIENT SHALE

ROCKY PLATEAU UNDERCUT BY EROSION

SALTBUSH SHRUBS IN AN ERODED GULLY

STREAKS OF PRAIRIE GRASS NEAR BIGFOOT PASS

ERODED ROCK FORMS IN NORTH DAKOTA'S BADLANDS

PUFFS OF WESTERN SALSIFY IN A SWEEP OF PRAIRIE

EVENING LIGHT ON THE DESOLATION OF NORBECK PASS

TIME
LIFE
BOOKS ®

Other Publications:
WORLD WAR II
THE GREAT CITIES
HOME REPAIR AND IMPROVEMENT
THE WORLD'S WILD PLACES
THE TIME-LIFE LIBRARY OF BOATING
HUMAN BEHAVIOR
THE ART OF SEWING
THE OLD WEST
THE EMERGENCE OF MAN
THE TIME-LIFE ENCYCLOPEDIA OF GARDENING
LIFE LIBRARY OF PHOTOGRAPHY
THIS FABULOUS CENTURY
FOODS OF THE WORLD
TIME-LIFE LIBRARY OF AMERICA
TIME-LIFE LIBRARY OF ART
GREAT AGES OF MAN
LIFE SCIENCE LIBRARY
THE LIFE HISTORY OF THE UNITED STATES
TIME READING PROGRAM
LIFE NATURE LIBRARY
LIFE WORLD LIBRARY
FAMILY LIBRARY:
  HOW THINGS WORK IN YOUR HOME
  THE TIME-LIFE BOOK OF THE FAMILY CAR
  THE TIME-LIFE FAMILY LEGAL GUIDE
  THE TIME-LIFE BOOK OF FAMILY FINANCE

THE BADLANDS

THE AMERICAN WILDERNESS/TIME-LIFE BOOKS/ALEXANDRIA, VIRGINIA

BY CHAMP CLARK
AND THE EDITORS OF TIME-LIFE BOOKS

Time-Life Books Inc.
is a wholly owned subsidiary of
TIME INCORPORATED

FOUNDER: Henry R. Luce 1898-1967

Editor-in-Chief: Hedley Donovan
Chairman of the Board: Andrew Heiskell
President: James R. Shepley
Vice Chairman: Roy E. Larsen
Corporate Editor: Ralph Graves

TIME-LIFE BOOKS INC.
MANAGING EDITOR: Jerry Korn
Executive Editor: David Maness
Assistant Managing Editors: Dale M. Brown, Martin Mann,
John Paul Porter
Art Director: Tom Suzuki
Chief of Research: David L. Harrison
Director of Photography: Melvin L. Scott
Planning Director: Philip W. Payne
Senior Text Editor: Diana Hirsh
Assistant Art Director: Arnold C. Holeywell
Assistant Chief of Research: Carolyn L. Sackett

CHAIRMAN: Joan D. Manley
President: John D. McSweeney
Executive Vice Presidents: Carl G. Jaeger (U.S. and Canada),
David J. Walsh (International)
Vice President and Secretary: Paul R. Stewart
Treasurer and General Manager: John Steven Maxwell
Business Manager: Peter G. Barnes
Sales Director: John L. Canova
Public Relations Director: Nicholas Benton
Personnel Director: Beatrice T. Dobie
Production Director: Herbert Sorkin
Consumer Affairs Director: Carol Flaumenhaft

THE AMERICAN WILDERNESS
Editorial Staff for *The Badlands*:
EDITOR: Robert Morton
Text Editors: Marion Buhagiar, Peter Janssen
Picture Editor: Jane D. Scholl
Designer: Charles Mikolaycak
Staff Writers: Sally Clark, Carol Clingan,
Simone D. Gossner, John von Hartz
Chief Researcher: Martha T. Goolrick
Researchers: Terry Drucker, Villette Harris, Beatrice Hsia,
Trish Kiesewetter, Mary Carroll Marden, Maggie Poucher
Design Assistant: Vincent Lewis

EDITORIAL PRODUCTION
Production Editor: Douglas B. Graham
Operations Manager: Gennaro C. Esposito
Assistant Production Editor: Feliciano Madrid
Quality Control: Robert L. Young (director),
James J. Cox (assistant), Michael G. Wight (associate)
Art Coordinator: Anne B. Landry
Copy Staff: Susan B. Galloway (chief), Barbara Quarmby,
Florence Keith, Celia Beattie
Picture Department: Dolores A. Littles, Joan Lynch

CORRESPONDENTS: Elisabeth Kraemer (Bonn); Margot Hapgood,
Dorothy Bacon (London); Susan Jonas, Lucy T. Voulgaris
(New York); Maria Vincenza Aloisi, Josephine du Brusle
(Paris); Ann Natanson (Rome). Valuable assistance was also
provided by Carolyn T. Chubet (New York).

The Author: Champ Clark, a Missourian, began his writing career as a reporter for *The Kansas City Star*. Subsequently he spent more than 20 years with TIME as a writer, editor, senior correspondent and chief of the Chicago news bureau. For this book, he made four trips to the Badlands, including one in which he lived for two months on the banks of the White River in the Pine Ridge Indian Reservation.

The Cover: Raked by warm afternoon light, the elephant-hide flanks of clay slopes in Badlands National Monument recede toward the sharp pinnacles of Castle Butte. The violent rainstorms, baking sun and winter ice characteristic of this part of the Dakotas have stripped the hills of vegetation, gullied their sides and cracked their surfaces. Confronted with such a landscape, men since earliest times — Sioux Indians, French trappers and white settlers — have called this area the badlands.

Contents

1/ World of the Westerly Wind   20
T. R., Tall in the Saddle   34
2/ Where Ancient Rivers Ran   42
A Swift Victory by Erosion   54
3/ Thunderhorse and Other Relics   70
A Nature Walk up Coyote Creek   82
4/ A Badlands Bestiary   94
The Sociable Prairie Dog   108
5/ The Bountiful Grasses   124
A Rich Mosaic of Growing Things   138
6/ An Untamable Terrain   154
June in the North   166

Bibliography   100
Acknowledgments and Credits   181
Index   182

The Ravaged Remains of a Prairie

Along a narrow strip at the edge of the Great Plains, in the western areas of North and South Dakota, lie the fiercely eroded remnants of ancient grassland known as the Badlands. Within the region—tinted on the detailed relief map at right—the most dramatic examples of nature's erosive forces can be found in Badlands National Monument in southwest South Dakota. There, the Great Wall—a colorful 200-foot-high slope—bisects the area.

A cousin of these Badlands is an irregular swath of eroded terrain along the Little Missouri River in North Dakota, where Teddy Roosevelt lived the life of a cowboy: the area is now a national park named for him.

On this map, the earth-cutting rivers and streams are shown as blue lines. Elevation is indicated by color—green in the river valleys, yellow for the grassy tablelands and white for the Black Hills. Mountain peaks and buttes are marked by black triangles; passes through the Great Wall are indicated by reversed parentheses. Red lines encompass national grasslands, Indian reservations and many other federally supervised areas where prairie dogs share their wilderness backyards with buffalo and pronghorn antelopes.

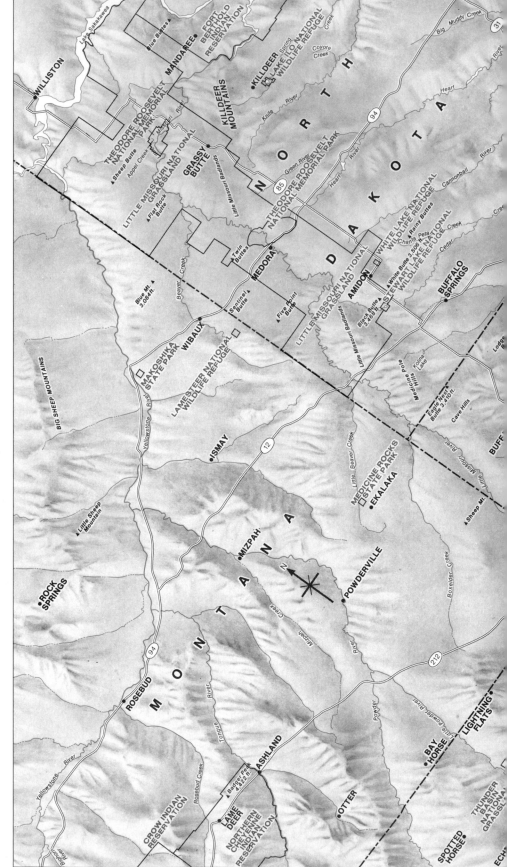

1/ World of the Westerly Wind

An' the prairie an' the butte-tops an' the long winds,
when they blow,
Is like the things what Adam knew on his birthday, long ago.

ANONYMOUS/ MEDORA NIGHTS

May has ended and one of the driest Junes in the history of this parched wilderness has begun. The day is hot—98° F. on a late afternoon—and the eternal wind from the west is blowing, dry and dusty. For two weeks this wind has been carrying fluffy white cottonwood seeds down the valley of the White River, creating a benign springtime blizzard. The only sounds are the whisper of the wind and the rattle of leaves on the cottonwood trees that line the river's banks. The wide riverbed is dry, except for a narrow streak of slow-running, milky water. A glare of white light reflects from the dun-colored clay. On both sides of the shallow stream, the clay has jelled into ripples, or baked hard into a craze of fine, broken lines. I am standing on the course of that dry river, and as I peer through the swirling seed storm, I see all around me the misshapen, tawny forms of the South Dakota Badlands.

This lonely place on the White River where I stand is, in fact, at the heart of the Badlands. And the drowsy afternoon is a relatively gentle interlude in the life of a harsh and brutal place. Over the millennia, this river and its neighbors have again and again erupted in floodwaters that have torn up the land through which they flow, creating battered monuments of multicolored strata, fluted walls of tan rock, and whimsical towers of clay and grass. On and off, over 20 million years, these streams have eroded a 6,000-square-mile tract of rock from the great grassland plain that sweeps across the middle of the continent.

The awesome natural excavation begins about 100 miles west of the Missouri River and continues on for 100 miles to the Black Hills. This band of ruined countryside, some 20 to 50 miles wide, embraces the basin of the White River north to the upland prairie on the south bank of the Bad River. The rains here are rare but hard, and the rocks are frail. In a few places, tough grasses cling tenaciously to the earth—only to be washed away when the treacherous rock beneath the sod gives way to the rush of water.

It is a confusing land, a disturbing land, full of strange and scalded shapes. Badlands.

It would be unthinkable to call them anything else. To the Dakota Indians they were *mako* (land) *sica* (bad), created by a powerful spirit of nature, Wakan Tanka, in a cataclysmic storm that sundered the earth when tribes from the Western mountains threatened to invade the plains. The storm left a barren swath on which, according to the legend, nothing has ever grown or can grow. And so, Wakan Tanka hoped, this part of the buffalo hunting ground would never again be fought over. Tough 18th Century French-Canadian fur trappers, who were probably the first whites to cross this part of the Dakotas, described the area as *les mauvaises terres à traverser*—bad lands to travel across. To present-day South Dakotans this bold wilderness of rock and grass, carved by water and dried by the westerly wind, is simply and proudly the Big Badlands.

There are other, smaller enclaves of badlands in this part of the continent. In North Dakota lies a forbidding region, of obvious kinship, where Teddy Roosevelt slew bison and tried unsuccessfully to run two cattle ranches. In fact, many of the rivers and streams that flow eastward through the Dakota plains to the Missouri have created isolated patches of erosion, stark enough to be called badlands. At the western end of South Dakota, however, lie mile after mile of *the* Badlands—my Badlands—the Badlands of which I have become, on relatively short acquaintance, both proud and jealous. They assault the senses. They affront sensibility. They are the biggest and the baddest.

The rivers that created the Badlands, usually so sluggish and clay-laden, often dry in summer and frozen in winter, are wild and powerful after spring thaws and summer storms. Such rivers have been hurling their strength against this plain for as long as the Black Hills and the Rockies have loomed over the land to the west. Beginning 35 million years ago, ancestral streams, born in the Western mountains, first created the plain by carrying down and depositing countless bits and pieces of granite, sandstone and limestone until the once-lofty Black Hills were surrounded by their own rocky detritus. Out of that level and gradually grassed-over deposit, newer rivers then carved the Badlands; the streams are still cutting into those ancient layers—sculpting the sandstone and shaping the clay.

Today, the three principal river systems that tear at the Big Badlands differ somewhat from each other in character, but their effect on the countryside is much the same. Along the Badlands' northwestern border, the Cheyenne River has chewed its way through the outwash from the Black Hills and has reached the underlying rock. The Cheyenne itself is now a fairly peaceful river, contained by hills on both sides of its course. However, the upland creeks that feed into it from the southeast are tempestuous and unpredictable, and they are still reducing the plain to naked barrens.

On the northern boundary, the Bad River meanders across a plain that is more grass than rock. The river is aptly named; its narrow channel is dry most of the year but floods swiftly and dangerously. As a result, the river's tributaries have crisscrossed the wide prairie on the south bank into gentle hummocks.

Finally, there is the White River, sometimes twisting sluggishly through a braided network of channels, other days roaring ominously as a united torrent, on its long course to the Missouri River. The White and its tributaries are the dominant erosional force in the Badlands. And like so many of the other features hereabouts, no one who has ever seen the White could call it anything else; its water is a dirty, chalky white, filled with clay particles that refuse to settle.

I started my first trip west to the Badlands on a soft, warm morning in May, leaving from the rich farmland of eastern South Dakota. The bucolic look of the countryside on the day-long journey did little to prepare me for a confrontation with another world. At first, the road I followed was lined for mile after uninterrupted mile with fields of corn and then of wheat, barley and oats. Farther west, high grass waved languorously on gentle, undulating slopes. The day wore on. Nothing much changed—except the grass, which became shorter.

Then I grew increasingly aware of the steady wind from the west, bending the grass toward the earth. I was moving into that part of the continent where the wind blows from the west almost without interruption for 11 or even 12 months of the year. It is a dry wind, one that has traveled a long way, dropped its burden of moisture as it crossed

Two expansive sod tables rise like stair treads

from Sage Creek Basin. The foreground terrace is approximately 12 feet high; Hay Butte, in the distance, climbs another 70 to 100 feet.

over the Western mountains from the Sierra to the Rockies and then swooped down across the plain.

This wind dominates the Western prairie. When rain does fall here, the hot, dry westerly quickly evaporates the moisture from the open land, as it was now blotting up the drops of perspiration that formed on my face in the afternoon sun. The first white settlers who moved onto the open grassland guessed that fires had burned off an original tree cover, but in fact the natural forces that keep the prairie free of forest are the lack of adequate precipitation plus the same dehydrating wind that blew against my face that day.

To prevent myself from being lulled to sleep by the relentless monotony of grass and wind, I began reckoning distance by fenceposts. Each post—or so it seemed—was a perch for a red-winged blackbird. At the approach of man or machine, the birds took off with a crimson flourish; often they were blown backward by the wind.

More miles and minutes passed, but still I saw no sign of badlands. The terrain remained gentle, comfortable. Just west of the small, dusty town of Kadoka, I glimpsed the first hint of something else; a craggy eminence appeared briefly on the horizon to the southwest. But its shape was vague—and soon blocked from my view by a gentle rise in the meadow to my left.

Twenty miles beyond Kadoka, just as I turned south, a low, jagged line appeared on the horizon, dark against the orange light of the late-afternoon sun. This time the disturbing and puzzling hint of torn landscape stayed in view. The rolling grassland terrain began to deteriorate, though slowly, without drama. Now, on my right, the prairie surface was becoming broken and blemished by low outcroppings of bare, beige rock. On my left, shallow gullies appeared on a low slope, tracing the paths of nameless streams now dry; heat waves shimmered above their baked clay beds. I stopped to scramble down one brick-hard bank, attempting to follow the course of the stream. It was impossible. At one point the stream bed split into five separate branches, which reconverged farther on.

Traces of smaller streams joined the main channel helter-skelter on both sides. I came to a place where the crisscrossing waters had gouged a lopsided checkerboard pattern from the floodplain. Each square of the checkerboard was a sheer-sided, 12-foot-high island of tan clay, sand and gravel about 30 feet wide and topped by a thatch of green grass. In their rain-swollen rushes, the streams had cut through the sur-

A dense layer of ground fog hangs in the valley of North Dakota's Little Missouri River the morning after a hard rain.

face and then into the more loosely compacted material below. Each torrent dug deeper, leaving ever-taller islands. Yet the same forces that had patiently elaborated this sculptured game board were also in the act of destroying it. Bit by bit, the crumbling base of each square was being undermined by rushing water. Inevitably, the towers would collapse and be washed away.

This was a fascinating testimony to the power and the intricacies of erosion. But Badlands? *The* Badlands? Disappointed and now bored by the day's minor revelations, I left the stream bed to continue driving south. I climbed up an easy, mile-long slope that continued around a gentle curve to the west.

Suddenly, as I blinked my eyes against the low-lying sun, the Badlands were there. Not on the horizon. Not a mile away, but just a few feet from me on the sharp slope that dipped off the left side of the road. They stretched toward the sun for as far as I could see—a wilderness of canyons, gullies, ridges, peaks and spires; a devil's den of colors that changed with each overpassing cloud. I stopped abruptly. Awe—and some fear—washed over me. I was at the very edge of a 200-foot precipice that plunged into a mammoth dissection of the earth's crust—a dissection that exposed all the frailty of that structure and, frailer still, the fossilized traces of life lived millions of years ago.

And I had not seen it until I was upon it.

I had been taken in by a grandiose trick of topography. The hulking, contorted shapes of the Badlands that I had expected to loom above me were actually *below* me. I was standing on a big peninsula of prairie grass jutting out above the basin of the White River. The river itself was a curling smear of white, barely identifiable some four miles away and 200 feet lower in elevation. Between the two levels of grassland lay a jagged slope of eroded rock, strewn with a great confusion of cliffs, buttes and ravines.

This ravaged strip is called the Great Wall of the Badlands. Actually it is not really a wall at all but rather the northern flank of the White River Basin, and it comprises the most spectacular and dramatic stretch of land sculpture in the entire area. Almost all the weathered and eroded buttes and pinnacles of the wall are lower than the upland plain out of which they have been cut. So it is possible to travel—as I did—along the upper grassland plain that stretched to the north and east and come, completely unaware, upon the startling vastness of the Badlands.

My first impression, as I stood on the wall's verge, was of utter chaos, of nature gone berserk. Rocks—an anarchy of rocks—were all that I could see; the desolation seemed complete. Then, as I continued to gaze into the abyss, I saw that there was life here. A dust-colored chipmunk scurried past my feet and down the steep slope, intent on some urgent task. Swallows darted and swooped through the air, chirping sharply. Isolated clumps of yucca and gray-green sage clung in splendid desperation to otherwise bare cliff faces. Grass—an extraordinary amount of grass—grew among the tumbled rocks. More grass carpeted every level place, even shadowed cliffside ledges and the wind-swept tops of buttes. Looking to the south, I could see a wide stretch of lush grassland spreading toward the tree-lined banks of the White River and beyond.

I soon found myself conjuring up shapes more recognizable and comforting than these raw Badlands crags—medieval castles with turrets and ramparts, pyramids, graceful minarets, church steeples. I was by no means the first to experience such architectural imaginings. For 150 years, venturers into the Badlands have attempted with varying success to express the impact of that first encounter with this mysterious act of creation. Almost without exception, the comparisons have been with structures built by man. In 1848, missionary Father Pierre Jean De Smet wrote: "Viewed at a distance, these lands exhibit the appearance of extensive villages and ancient castles, but under forms so extraordinary, and so capricious a style of architecture, that we might consider them as appertaining to some new world, or ages far remote." And in 1935, architect Frank Lloyd Wright: "What I saw gave me an indescribable sense of mysterious otherwhere—a distant architecture, ethereal, touched, only touched, with a sense of Egyptian. . . ."

But to find in the Badlands only the familiar shapes and forms of human civilization is to place unnatural limits on human imagination. In the Badlands the human scale of size and sense is easily lost. The sheer ruthlessness of a gully slashing sharply down off the level grassland magnifies the depth of the cut. Imagination soars, shaped only by the mood and the moment. Light and shadow play on the sharp, stark outlines of the land and confuse the eye. A cloud passes—and the graceful becomes the grotesque. What I see, or what I think I see, may completely escape a companion. What he sees, and marvels at, appears to me as something ordinary.

How wide that gulf can be was demonstrated to me later that summer. It was a dreadful July day, with the temperature up to 110° F. In late afternoon the great wind from the west rocketed through the Bad-

THE GEOLOGIC TIME SCALE

For many years experts have argued about the dates to be assigned to the eras, periods and epochs of the geologic time scale. The scale generally accepted for many years has been founded on one that was devised by J. Laurence Kulp of Columbia University. But more recently a scale compiled for the Elsevier Scientific Publishing Company has gained wide acceptance. The scale used here in this book is an updated Kulp scale; its relationship to the Elsevier scale can be seen below.

	DATE MILLIONS OF YEARS AGO	
	Kulp Scale	Elsevier Scale
Paleozoic Era		
Cambrian Period	600	570
Ordovician Period	500	500
Silurian Period	440	435
Devonian Period	400	395
Carboniferous Period		
Mississippian Epoch	350	345
Pennsylvanian Epoch	325	310
Permian Period	270	280
Mesozoic Era		
Triassic Period	225	230
Jurassic Period	180	195
Cretaceous Period	135	141
Cenozoic Era		
Tertiary Period		
Paleocene Epoch	70	65
Eocene Epoch	60	55
Oligocene Epoch	40	35
Miocene Epoch	25	22.5
Pliocene Epoch	10	5
Quaternary Period		
Pleistocene Epoch	2	1.8

lands at 50 miles per hour, obliterating the sun with clouds of dust and driving me into my tent-camper on the south bank of the White River. The gale died as suddenly as it was born, leaving behind a wake of dust particles that swirled on the horizon to create the most magnificent sunset I had ever seen.

To get a better view, I drove about half a mile west and then walked across a meadow to a bluff about 80 feet over the river. In the northwest sky, framed by rose-colored clouds, was a great mirage, an eerie mirror image of the Badlands that surrounded me. Every detail that glistened on the ground seemed to be reflected above: the twisting line of the White River, not chalky-white but silver; the grasslands to the north, not sere, as they were actually becoming, but deep emerald; even a sunlit outline of the Great Wall, peak by peak and spire by spire. I needed a witness. I raced back to the campground and persuaded the first person I met—the 13-year-old son of another camper —to return to the bluff with me, though I was afraid that by the time we got back, the illusion would be gone. But it wasn't. Eagerly, I pointed out to the confused boy feature after feature projected in the sky. The lad listened patiently, then looked at me as if I were somewhat odd and muttered, "Very pretty." I looked up again and the illusion had disappeared. It had been there. I know it. Or at least I think I know it.

For most people, the powerful grandeur and the beauty of the Badlands at any time of day is simply not a comfortable thing to look at. Visitors are impressed by the place, but they do not necessarily like it. About 1.3 million tourists annually pass through the Badlands National Monument of South Dakota, a national park area that encompasses only about 6 per cent of the Big Badlands. They spend an average of three and a half hours in the Monument area, giving them barely enough time for the first "oohs" and "ahs" over the starkness of the place and maybe a couple of stops at carefully constructed overlooks—or perhaps a short walk along a marked trail. Then, in the blaze and glare of a Badlands midafternoon, someone will look at his watch and say: "Well, they're bad all right. Let's get out of here." And on west they rush, to the Black Hills and Mount Rushmore, where they can throng with thousands of others to stare at four huge Presidential faces blasted out of granite—an engineering feat of the highest order but certainly not as spectacular as the natural wonder of the Badlands. The North Dakota Badlands are farther away from the traditional east-west tourist trek; some 853,000 tourists a year pass through Theodore Roosevelt National Memorial Park, and on the average, each spends only about two hours there before hastening on.

The Badlands climate, like the sunsets, sometimes exaggerates the forbidding aspects of the landscape. In 1850 a young man named Thaddeus Culbertson eagerly set out to explore the Badlands, financed by the Smithsonian Institution and by his brother, who built fur-trading posts on the Missouri. It was May when Culbertson camped alongside the White River and wrote: "Fancy yourself on the hottest day in summer, in the hottest spot of such a place without water, without an animal, and scarcely an insect astir, without a single flower to speak pleasant things to the eye, and you will have some idea of the utter loneliness of the Bad Lands."

Throughout the year, the climate in the Badlands remains one of extremes: hot and dry in summer, cold and dry in winter. Everything that might shelter the land from the harshness of sudden change is sparse here. Few clouds, let alone trees, exist to deflect the fierce rays of the summer sun. And little snow falls, so that the ground here is deprived of any protective cover during the piercing cold of winter. The humid Atlantic air, which nurtures the forests of the East and helps to temper climate along the coast, rarely reaches the Badlands. The parched westerly wind is what dominates the weather here. And when the westerly is especially strong, it penetrates farther and farther east. The Atlantic moisture remains farther east, and the result is the kind of extended drought that drove cattle ranchers and farmers out of the Badlands and off the Western plains during the 1930s.

Besides its extremes of drought and heat and cold, the Badlands climate is one of sudden and sometimes savage change. The annual average temperature of 48° F. does not even begin to reflect the historical spread of 158° between the record high of 116° F. in 1910 and the low of −42° F. in 1916. I endured a day in early July when the temperature fell from 111° at 4 p.m. to 49° at midnight—an eight-hour plunge of 62°. I went to sleep in my camp that night bathed in sweat; when I woke three hours later, I was shivering with cold, and I spent the rest of the night wrapped in a bedroll.

Storms in the area tend to be locally produced by just such quick rises and falls in temperature, and they are sharp in their impact. The rainfall they generate comes in sudden, ferocious inundations, not as carefully measured segments of the annual average of 16 inches.

Three times during one summer in the Badlands, I experienced the adventure of watching the elemental forces of water and wind attack and carve the earth's vulnerable mantle of rock and soil. The first time came late in the afternoon of a May day when a galaxy of storms was upon the land. Grim black clouds, driven by a gale force wind, raced over the Badlands so low that their bellies were pierced by the up-thrust spires and pinnacles. As if in pain and anger, the scudding clouds let loose jagged, smashing bolts of lightning. The thunder did not just peal. It cannonaded through ravines and gulches, shaking the ground. And there, on a wide cliff shelf of the Great Wall, I stood—thoroughly drenched and more than a little alarmed.

Folly had led me out there. I already knew that the Badlands are no-torious for the bewildering speed with which storms appear, disappear and move. And I had ignored this fact. I had also been deceived by a wide swath of blue sky directly above me, and had climbed onto a cliff near the eastern end of the wall to look south toward a storm that had suddenly appeared over the White River three miles away. As I watched, the sky cleared over the river valley. The grasslands, bathed first by rain and now by sun, stretched in freshened green to a line of cottonwood trees along the river's banks. In the opposite direction, north of the wall on the upland grass plain, a brilliant rainbow was on display. Captivated by the spectacle, I failed to notice that clouds had overtaken my own vantage point. I was plunged into sudden darkness and caught in a wild, torrential rain.

I was surprised but not frightened at first. The cliffside did not seem a likely place for a rockfall, and lightning has never bothered me. As the rain soaked the cliff, though, I suddenly became aware that the Bad-lands clay on which I was standing is, when wet, one of the earth's slick-est substances. With the wind shrieking around me, I had a sharp and vivid image of myself sliding right over the brink. I moved back against the cliff face, grabbed onto the branch of a juniper tree that had sur-vived many a storm and hung on grimly.

As I waited for a break in the storm, the cliffside against which I crouched and the valley just below me were transformed. Water from past storms had already eroded the cliff so that it was more wrinkled than an elephant's hide—and each tiny, natural wrinkle was now a wa-terway leading to the valley below. In that valley, the meadows were wildly agitated; rolling madly through them were streams that only min-utes ago had been dry beds. And each of those streams, by however cir-cuitous a route, was heading for the White River—on whose banks I had made my camp. I decided right then that my best plan was to get

The glow of an afternoon sun, vividly refracted in the dust and moisture of a storm front, lights the frost-hewn spires of Vulture Peak.

away from this place. When the rain let up for a bit, I cautiously made my way off the ledge and raced back to my car.

The second adventure followed from the first. A storm that had begun with a gods' race of speeding thunder chariots turned into three days and nights of steady, soaking wind-blown rain. More than one fourth the total precipitation that would fall on the Badlands that year fell within those 72 hours—a pattern not uncommon for the area. Before the rain began, the White River had been somnolent—dry across three quarters of its width and so shallow in most places that it could be waded across at ankle depth. But in those 72 drenching hours the river rose seven and a half feet, plunging east with gigantic energy carrying along the trunks of great cottonwood trees as though they were twigs.

The frothy torrent came within 18 inches of pouring over its banks onto the floodplain. These were my measurements, of course, but considering that my camp was on that plain, only about a dozen feet from the south bank, I took considerable care to be accurate. On the second day of the storm I committed a small environmental sin. I took an empty beer can, filled it with gravel, and planted it on the steep slope of the riverbank exactly a foot from the top. As soon as the beer can was swept away—and since sleep was difficult in the noisy turmoil of the storm, I checked at all sorts of odd hours—I was prepared to roll up my bedroll and leave.

At 4 o'clock on the third morning of the storm, the river crested within six inches of my beer can. By 8 a.m., when the rain finally stopped, the river was already down at least eight inches. I walked, somewhat bleary-eyed, away from the riverbank and met one of the other campers, who had spent the storm in a mobile home 300 yards from the water. "Gee," he said cheerfully, "I thought for a while last night you were going to take a ride down the river." I was less amused.

By noon, the water level was down about two feet and the crisis was over—for a while. Several weeks later, when the water had long returned to its usual torpid state, I left the campground one morning at 11 o'clock and returned three hours later to find the river again rising and surging although not a drop of rain had fallen in the near vicinity. There had been a cloudburst early that morning in the upland prairie some 40 miles to the west.

The final experience came at the end of June, more than a month after I had stood among the wind-blown cottonwood seeds on the bed of the White River. The heat was fierce—about 102° F.—but for some forgotten reason I decided to take a hike up the riverbed. There had been a heavy cloudburst a few days before; the river had surged, then rapidly receded again. The erosive effects of the storm were visible everywhere. Before, when I had walked here, I had stopped to rest on a small, solidly compacted promontory that jutted about four feet into the riverbed. Now it had washed away, without leaving a trace. Beneath a high bluff, a new fall of rock rested at the river's edge.

Farther upstream, some of the roots of a grand old cottonwood were laid bare for 20 feet or more along the low-lying riverbank. The tree would survive; cottonwood roots sometimes spread underground to cover an area larger than a basketball court. Nearby I was astonished to see three tiny cottonwood saplings that had managed to take root in the river channel. They had grown little stemlike trunks six to eight inches tall, and thrust out small, wiry branches—all in the six weeks or so since the May seed blow. During that time several torrents had rushed over the tiny cottonwoods, ripping up earth and rock all around them. But there they stood—all three thriving, with new leaves budding on the branches.

At the end of my walk up the river that day, I saw a mound of grayish-black rock exposed along the bank. I knew that I had not seen it there before, because this was a special kind of rock: shale. It is the foundation rock of the Badlands, the rock on which 1,000 feet of Black Hills sand and silt had been deposited and then carved away. The fact that this small patch of shale was exposed meant that at this place the White River had come to the end of its ferocious task of creating Badlands. And it had happened since my last walk along the river.

T. R., Tall in the Saddle

Theodore Roosevelt was born loving the outdoors, and dreaming of being a bully outdoorsman—like the hell-for-leather cowpuncher at right. He entered his avocation as a pale, asthmatic boy who walked the hills of New York's Adirondacks during the 1870s, reveling in the sight of the wilderness' creatures.

However, it was not until 1883, when he made his first trip out to the North Dakota Badlands, that T. R., by then a 24-year-old New York state legislator, got his chance to absorb himself in the great American wilderness.

Like many another buckskin adventurer to the West, Roosevelt set out to hunt buffalo. He detrained at Little Missouri in the Dakota Territory in September. But before he shot his first bull, he became so smitten by the whole area that he decided to take up ranching on the open range. Forthwith he signed a check for $14,000 to buy into a spread called the Maltese Cross, after the cattle's brand. The next year he increased his herds and built a second ranch he called Elkhorn.

In his own mind T. R. was now a fully breveted cattleman, and he proudly recorded—or had recorded for him—in the pictures preserved on the following pages, his delight in himself and the life he was leading. At the outset the local cowboys received the bustling, spectacled future President with unconcealed scorn. They called him Four-Eyes or Storm Windows. They noted his addiction to such uncowboy-like refinements as shaving or brushing his teeth. And they reacted with surprise to T. R.'s abstemious ways in a business where a good many hands drank up their wages.

Before long, however, the boisterous Roosevelt had showed he could stay with his horse on the roughest roundup, and even chase desperados (pages 40-41). When he abandoned the life of a full-time rancher after the winter of 1886-1887 to absorb himself once and for all in politics, the wild West lost a good hand—and one of its most passionate advocates.

But he left behind him a rich legacy, not only for the West but for all of outdoor America. As President, he oversaw the creation of four major national parks, proclaimed 16 national monuments, and established 51 bird reserves. And in 1947, the area of North Dakota where T. R. had had his most memorable outdoor adventure became Theodore Roosevelt National Memorial Park.

Duded up in buckskin and sporting a pistol, T. R. sits astride his favorite mount, Manitou.

Roosevelt's snapshot of the porch at the Elkhorn Ranch features a display of antlers from elk shot for meat by T. R. and his ranch hands.

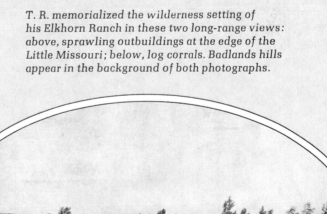

T. R. memorialized the wilderness setting of
his Elkhorn Ranch in these two long-range views:
above, sprawling outbuildings at the edge of the
Little Missouri; below, log corrals. Badlands hills
appear in the background of both photographs.

Sylvane Ferris, a manager of the Maltese
Cross Ranch, and two cow hands make ready
to saddle up at a temporary corral.
Each cowboy needed as many as 12 mounts
for roundup, changing horses often during a
working day that could last 18 hours.

An Indian ranch hand sits by and Ferris
watches from his horse, while the cook loads
his chuck wagon during roundup. Roosevelt,
who loved the work, said, "There
is more excitement in the roundup than
in politics. And it is far more respectable."

The climax to Teddy Roosevelt's adventure in the wild West occurred in the spring of 1886, when three local toughs stole the only boat that T. R. kept on the riverfront at Elkhorn Ranch. Knocking together a flat-bottomed scow, T. R. and two fellow cow men pushed off in pursuit. On the third morning, the President-to-be surprised and quickly subdued the thieves (right). A triumphant Roosevelt snapped the picture above of his two deputies, the bearded Bill Sewall and Will Dow, then dragged the dejected felons to jail. En route the proud Teddy was somewhat bemused when, far from being praised for his feat, he was confronted by an old rancher who asked why Roosevelt had made "all this fuss instead of hanging 'em offhand."

2/ Where Ancient Rivers Ran

*A story of strange climate, strange geography...of a varied
series of events through ages and ages of time showing
the working-out of well-laid plans with no human being
to help or interfere.* CLEOPHAS C. O'HARRA/ *THE WHITE RIVER BADLANDS*

Time and again during the seasons I spent in the Badlands, I found
myself unsettled by the constant wind, the sudden changes in temperature, the uneasy footing on the crumbling rock and the sharp,
unexpected angles of the land. At such times, I retreated from the tu-
multuous vistas into those parts of the Badlands where I could feel the
earth at rest. One favorite place was the softly swelling plain around
Sage Creek. Another was the lofty, grass-covered top of Sheep Mountain Table. Less than 20 miles separate these two gentling prospects of
land; yet the top of the table, with its spectacular view of the jagged
Badlands, is some 800 feet higher than the creek basin—not quite so
high as some of the hills of San Francisco. The dimensions themselves
are not striking, but Sage Creek is in the basement of the Badlands and
the table is the roof.

These facts generate a paradox, a seeming contradiction to the sense
of peace I discover in those places. For surrounding the two calm and
restful sites lie 120 million years of tempestuous earth history—years
in which a great sea came and went, and mountains rose and then crumbled to create the layers of rock out of which the Badlands were then
carved. The story of what happened here is not extraordinary—at least
not by the standards of geologists who have learned to deal with infin-
ities of time and the strenuous churnings of the earth's crust. The
distinction of the Badlands is that here, erosion has revealed a history

that the earth usually keeps well hidden. A visitor like myself, armed with nothing more than a measure of curiosity, a comfortable pair of hiking shoes and a canteen full of water, can pick up and hold in his hands the evidence of these eons.

I had my first introduction to that ancient chronicle while trying to track down traces of much more recent events. The first time I explored Sage Creek, which meanders in a scooped-out section of terrain between the Great Wall and the upland plain of the Badlands, I was searching for an old Indian trail and fur traders' route last used with any regularity in the 1850s by the United States Army. Recently, a young naturalist with the National Park Service spent more than a year hiking and riding her horse over the hillocks and rim of Sage Creek Basin trying to identify the old track that had crossed the area from Fort Pierre on the Missouri River to Fort Laramie, 300 miles to the southwest. Someone had shown me a copy of the map she made, and I penciled the route on my own map and set out, in a casual way, to walk that historic road for a few miles.

I quickly became discouraged, however. The grass I trampled yielded no detectable mark of the abandoned road. So I gave up and struck out across a field toward a curve in the creek that curled up against a hill of gray-black rock. The creek was only a few feet wide at the base of the dark cliff, and it was moving so sluggishly that a wet crust of tan clay coated the surface of the water. The dark bluff rose abruptly for 60 feet or so to a crown of grass, and the entire cliff face described a shallow curve that matched the bend of the creek. The whole place seemed like a quiet cove on an island shore—an invitation to rest.

When I reached the creek, I noticed the fragments of a large boulder on the dry edge of the white clay creek bed. The gray-black color of the shattered rock was the same as the cliff's. I bent down to look more closely at the biggest fragment—a large, bowl-shaped piece. I ran my fingers along the curved sides of the dull-faced rock; it had the densely porous feel of a slate blackboard. This was, in fact, shale—the age-old, compacted sediment made of disintegrated rock and decayed organic matter that once had been the black ooze at the bottom of a sea.

The thought struck with considerable impact. Here I was 2,500 feet above sea level, 1,100 miles from the nearest ocean, in the dry and dusty Badlands—standing amid the remains of an ancient sea. Here in my hands was the evidence of a major flooding of the interior of the North American continent that had begun more than 100 million years ago. An arm of the Arctic Ocean had probed south across the land, finally meeting waters flooding north from the Gulf Coast. The result was a shallow, muddy sea that covered 1,000 miles from the flanks of volcanoes in the west to a gentle shoreline in the east, located about where the iron-ore boats dock today in Duluth, Minnesota. Approximately 1,500 feet of black, mucky sea bottom had covered the section of the Badlands on which I was standing, entombing millions of sea lizards and snails, mammoth fish, giant clams and ammonites. Then, over ensuing millions of years, as the earth arched upward gently, the sea slowly drained into the Gulf of Mexico. And the dark mud of the bottom dried and was transformed into the dark shale that now makes up the basement of the Badlands.

This memento of the great flood—called Pierre shale by geologists—underlies much of the Great Plains. In places along the Missouri, so much organic matter was trapped and later covered over that the shale may someday be an economical source of petroleum: oil is generated from decayed animal and plant matter buried deep in the earth. But the shards of rock in my hands on that dry morning were neither practical nor useful. With their dark origin so evident, for me they were simply a gift of the wilderness.

As I looked up at the shale cliff itself, I realized the surface that had looked so solid from afar was actually a skin composed of tiny fragments of broken rubble. The hard rains of the Badlands had penetrated the rock; the gases and chemicals that make up the air and water were weathering it into flakes, eventually to become sand and silt that would be carried away by Sage Creek. I dug into the cliffside and tore off a handful of the crumbling rock; that small gesture triggered a rockslide that zipped down 12 feet of the cliff face as explosively as if I had lighted a fuse. Hundreds of such probes by the swollen floodwaters of Sage Creek have produced the womblike hollow that I had noticed as I approached and that I would see again and again in the hills of shale at Sage Creek and elsewhere in the Badlands.

Similar weathering and erosion had attacked the dry bed of the ancient sea in the long, warm seasons of those bygone years. Seeds blew into the crumbled rock from trees and flowering plants surrounding the area. A swampy jungle of trees, ferns and shrubs covered the plain. The same eons-long arching of the earth's crust that had drained the sea forced a mass of granitic rock up toward the surface west of the Badlands. Mantled by ancient sea sediments, the 7,500-foot dome of rock rose above the undulating plain. The Black Hills were born.

Cracked open when it tumbled into a creek bed, this colorful object—called a concretion—reveals its innards of black shale shot through with the orange mineral siderite. Concretions form inside sedimentary rocks when their minerals collect around a small foreign body, much in the way that a pearl forms within an oyster.

As the hills went up, a series of faults extended out into the plain to the east. A ridge about 150 feet high formed along one of those faults, just north of where I stood that morning at Sage Creek. The ridge continued east for another 30 miles or so. To the south a higher, steep-sided escarpment paralleled the northern ridge for 60 miles, running into present-day Nebraska. And between these two high ridges a flat-bottomed valley about five miles wide was formed—a valley carved by the first river of the Badlands.

This broad river valley was never seen by man. It was the home of turtles, alligators, prehistoric lizards and a variety of early mammals. But the valley has been given a name by John Clark (no relation of mine), a determined geologist from the Field Museum of Natural History in Chicago, who spent 40 years studying the Badlands. Clark called the ancient stretch between ridges the Red River Valley—not because it reminded him in any way of the valley between Texas and Oklahoma made famous by cowboy ballads, but because the black shale of the ancient sea bed through which the river flowed was transformed into red soil. For 30 million years, warm rains drenched the valley, mixing together the rubble of flaking rock and the remains of lush vegetation. Waters made acid by carbon dioxide and plant decay leached and dissolved the grains of rock into new soil; the white calcium carbonate in the shale washed away, the proportion of iron and aluminum oxides increased, and the earth turned a rusty red.

I saw that red soil less than an hour after I found the shale along Sage Creek. I was following the creek east. At first, the land on the northern bank rippled into a grassy plain. Soon, though, colored mounds of earth 20 to 40 feet high loomed over the grass. The top layer, perhaps three feet thick, glowed darkly red and umber; beneath, the naked layers of rock merged into yellowish browns, brownish purples and finally into the gray black of the now-familiar Pierre shale.

I climbed the sliding, weathered surface of one of the mounds, my search for the old abandoned Army road now long forgotten as I realized that I was probably standing on the eroded northern ridge of the Red River Valley. In this place, the dusty red layer at the top was all that remained of the rich deep soil of that upland ridge, which had once sustained a thick green mantle of flowering shrubs and now was only sparsely vegetated with grass and stunted shrubbery.

From that day on I never climbed a hill or walked along a creek bed of the Badlands without looking for remains of that valley and signs of its history. A few days later I was again clambering up and down the slopes of some ancient soil in a more eastern section of the Badlands, when I noticed a small field with curiously uniform gravel scattered across its ruddy surface. I bent down and picked up a few pieces, which glinted in the sunlight. The pebbles were all rounded and polished with what looked like shiny lacquer.

Once, these rocks had been mixed with pebbles made of softer stuff —feldspar, sandstone, limestone—that washed down from the Black Hills. Harsh weathering and the downstream tumble had destroyed the more vulnerable rocks entirely, but the acid waters had only succeeded in smoothing, polishing and reducing the size of the specially hard specimens I found—quartz, jasper and chert—that had been torn from the granitic core of the Black Hills. This sprawl of gleaming pebbles was the vanguard of a mysterious, incompletely understood event that overtook the Red River and buried the ancient valley.

A clue to what may have happened lies in the gently sloped, elongated, haystack-shaped humps of pale, green- and pink-tinted gray rock that undulate softly and irregularly out of the plain south of the Great Wall. A long line of these moody rock waves stretches northeast of Sheep Mountain Table; indeed, the hillocks emerge from the grassland of creek basins all through the Badlands. They mark the course of the Red River and its valley. The clay, silt, sand and volcanic ash that make up the formations were churned together when the tributaries of the Red River, rushing down from the Black Hills, suddenly turned into torrents. The waters ripped away at the outer layers of sediment on the mountains and tore more deeply into the hard core. First, the pebbles were thrown down onto the red earth of the valley. Floods then poured down the lower slopes of the mountains, dumping quantities of red and green clays into the valley and adding this colorful muddy burden in layers on top of the earlier deposits of gravel.

A change in climate probably caused the flooding. For millions of years warm, drenching monsoonal rains, originating in the north, had fallen each summer directly on the Red River Valley. But about 40 million years ago the earth's poles cooled and new global weather patterns developed. Chief among the changes was that the wind flow over the area now shifted, and rain-bearing clouds from the west poured their burden of water onto the slopes of the Black Hills. The mountain creeks filled with mud and silt into which was mixed volcanic ash that had drifted down from the newly erupting Rockies farther west, and washed the mixture of debris eastward into the valley of the Red River.

The downpour of deposits continued almost without interruption for three or four million years. Muddy sediments finally lapped over the weathered ridges of the old valley and spilled onto the swampy plains that lay to the north and south. Then, as the valley was filled and its contours obliterated, the rivers coming down off the mountains abated and the land came to rest once more.

When I walked around and between the crumbling humps of rock, which geologists call the Chadron Formation, I was walking through the eroded remains of the Red River Valley's death mask—an impression molded from the muddy inundation as it dried out and was compacted by later overburdens of rock that have since washed away. What startled me every time I came close to the humps was the fact that anything so vulnerable to air and water could have lasted so long. The surface of the humps is a slipping, sliding mantle of broken clay; I usually had to crawl up the last few feet on my hands and knees. When wet, the clay turns immediately into a soggy gel that slumps down the sides. More out of playful curiosity than serious inquiry, I took a handful of surface clay from a hump soon after the rain stopped one afternoon and squeezed out a long dribble of milky-white water.

My hikes in the Badlands were now motivated by a fresh purpose, and I knew that nearly anything I touched, kicked or squeezed could add to my awareness of the area's ancient history. One day I found hidden atop a Chadron hump a fragile token of the interlude of peace following the muddy deluge that had filled the Red River Valley. I was again on the road that passed through the Chadron Formation northeast of Sheep Mountain Table, when I spotted a whitish slab of rock, distinguishable more by its shape than by its color, jutting out slightly from the curved top of one of the humps. I scrambled up, sat carefully on the sliding slope and looked at what turned out to be fine-textured limestone about a foot thick. After I brushed away a litter of clay dust and fragments, I poured a tiny bit of water from my canteen onto the rock to see it more clearly. The water sank immediately into the delicate pores of the white rock, which had been formed in part from the pulverized shells of fresh-water snails. And in the damp splash mark I could even discern some complete, fossilized shells of these ancient snails—a half dozen or so, none longer than a quarter of an inch.

I was, in fact, sitting on the site of a long-extinct, swampy pond formed in that tranquil time when a wooded plain had newly established itself atop the buried remains of the Red River Valley. The waters

So thick with mud that it oozes rather than flows, Sage Creek gives no hint of the erosive force of waters that once poured through this valley, scouring the overlying sediments and cutting deeply into the underpinnings of Pierre shale. In this view, the striated cliff at center is Pierre shale eroded and redeposited by the ancient waters, which also left bands of light-colored sediment washed off surrounding slopes. The dark bank at the far right is Pierre shale, too, carried down to the creek's edge by rain and runoff.

that then flowed softly out of the Black Hills neither cut down, nor built up, the plain of trees and other flowering plants that stretched almost flat from the base of the mountains east to Kadoka, north to Wall and south toward Nebraska. Algae lived and died on the bottoms of the pools of water; snails crawled along the pond beds feeding on the algae; primitive horses the size of large dogs nibbled at the leaves of surrounding shrubs. The peace lasted for tens of thousands of years. But during all those millennia, an element of change continued: the climate. The nearby Black Hills captured increasing amounts of moisture from the winds blowing steadily out of the west, and the plain, now inhabited by giant pigs and rhinoceroses, grew more and more arid. It was getting cooler too. The change was not continuous and steady. The arid periods got longer, the humid periods shorter; dry stretches were followed by sudden episodes of heavy rainfall.

The effect was cumulative—and devastating to the forested plain. Streams that had flowed clear and languidly toward the east became roiling, engulfing sweeps of mud. The pigs and rhinoceroses wallowing in the river were unceremoniously buried in the advancing floods. The sediments spread out in clearly defined layers. When there was less rain in the Black Hills, the rivers brought down only fine clay and silty substances; when the downpour was torrential and protracted, coarse-textured layers of sand were deposited. Where the creeks tore iron oxide from the slopes, the layers were tinted pink; traces of manganese dioxide, the same mineral that turns some old glass violet, saturated sections of deposited mud with shades of lavender. More and more ash from the volcanoes in the Rockies washed down with the streams, blanching the mud with its ghastly pallor. One fall of ash, blasted high into the air and blown eastward on the prevailing winds, was so heavy that it left a coherent, stark-white layer up to 55 feet thick.

The Chadron Formation and the plain that had developed and flourished over it were buried under 500 feet of debris. These layered bands of sediment, now revealed in the jagged slopes of the Great Wall and the stately buttes and pillars of rock that stand above the White River grassland, are the totems of the Badlands, a reminder of the ancestry of the place and the character that marks them.

East of Sheep Mountain Table, erosion has cut down through the layers, deep into the Chadron Formation immediately below and into the Pierre shale below that. The eloquence of these mammoth cross sections is no greater to me, though, than the bits and pieces of rock that I

Eroded into the shape of a lumbering centipede, this mound of compacted clay, sand, gravel and volcanic ash supports a wisp of sod.

picked up on my walks: mudstone, for instance. Was there ever a homelier name for a rock? I found it in all kinds of murky colors in the Badlands—nondescript gray, yellow tan, rusty red. And almost every piece had the same abundant array of tiny, dull-edged particles frozen within it in wild disorder—fragments of Black Hills rock mixed in the viscous flow of the runoff that had rolled onto the plain.

The accumulation of such bits and pieces eventually resulted some five million years ago in a lofty, grassy plain that rose as high as 5,500 feet above sea level and stretched north to Alberta, Canada, east toward the present Mississippi Valley, and south to the high plains of New Mexico and Texas, where the grass still grows on an uneroded surface of mud and dust.

In the Badlands, however, profound erosion during that time ripped away at the previously deposited sediments on a scale and at a pace that inspires awe. First, the mountain-bred rivers began sweeping the rocky sediment from the Badlands area into the creeks flowing toward the Missouri River. Then, one million years ago, the ice age began. While glaciers never scoured the Badlands, dark clouds generated by the same cooling climate that created the glaciers in the north poured rain into the area. Shallow rivers that were the size of lakes formed, sprawling as much as six miles wide; but for all their expanse, they raced along the plain at speeds as high as 15 miles an hour, leaving a glittering wake of calico-patterned jasper, spotted agates, garnets, tourmalines, quartz and other gemstones from the Black Hills. (The gravel fields near the White River Basin towns of Imlay and Interior have been foraged by generations of rock hounds without being depleted.) The area grew more arid as the climate of the whole northern hemisphere warmed. Today, though the rivers are much smaller, erosion has resumed, with a predictable result—jagged badlands.

On my first trip to Sheep Mountain Table, the highest spot in Badlands National Monument, I had looked around, innocently satisfied that I had reached the end of my quest for the origins of the Badlands. But, of course, I had not. Another 500 feet or so of rock had once reached up to the wide sky above this table, and then were eroded away. Sheep Mountain Table is being whittled down at a rate that geologists regard as ferocious—though on my tiny human time scale, the grassy, juniper-rimmed table seems peaceful enough.

One summer's afternoon I climbed again to the top of the table and walked across a narrow bridge of land to the southern end. A family of Indians had just finished their dinner on the grass, and I was reminded that I had crossed over into the Oglala Sioux reservation. The young children were playing with a Frisbee. I looked on for a time and then remembered a discovery I had made some weeks before: how to pluck "carrot sticks" out of volcanic ash. If I picked the right spot, just at the edge of the table where the grass ended and the brittle festoons of white ash began, I found small circles—perfectly round, no bigger than a thumbprint and slightly darker than the surrounding rock. I walked to the place, sat down and gently ran the point of my pocketknife around the edge of one of the circles. Then I lifted out an almost perfect three-inch-long rock cylinder: my carrot stick. I cracked it open by striking it with the knife handle and found a toothpick-sized hole inside, glittering with tiny blue-white zeolite crystals, a group of minerals often found in lava flows. Probably when the ash blew to this place 25 million years ago from the erupting Rockies, imprisoned water vapor or carbon dioxide escaped upward, formed that tiny hole, and slightly altered the chemistry of the ash to create my little carrot stick; then zeolite crystals grew in the interior hollow. Perhaps that is what happened. No one really knows.

I looked down into the gloomy wilderness of grotesque and graceful rock—all of it doomed. Around me, and resting casually in my hand, was the evidence and memory of violence, of rock and soil vomited from the earth, blown by the wind, churned by turbulent waters. Yet, as twilight fell on the grass, the table top became a place of cathedral silence, a place to sit quietly and enjoy the present, a place to set up camp and spend the night in peace.

A Swift Victory by Erosion

PHOTOGRAPHS BY ENRICO FERORELLI

No wild region of North America demonstrates the ravaging forces of erosion more dramatically than the Big Badlands of South Dakota, where geological change has happened so rapidly that the evolution of land forms seems to have occurred in a speeded-up movie film.

The Badlands came to their present state of magnificent ruin in a mere five million years. Today the process of quick disintegration continues as the Badlands crumble under the attack of running water, abetted by an unforgiving climate. Many Badlands hills are being cut down at the rate of about a half inch per year. By comparison, the Mississippi River Basin north of Baton Rouge drops little more than an inch in 1,000 years.

A main factor in the fast-paced devastation of the Badlands is the unusual softness of their underlying rocks. Though here and there an outcropping of tough sandstone occurs, the dominant rocks are as yielding as their names—mudstone and siltstone—suggest. Mostly hard to the touch when dry but easily broken up by water, they were laid down as sediments by ancestral rivers.

These soft rocks provided the perfect raw material for the sharp sculpting tools of nature. About five million years ago the tools went to work with a vengeance. Dominated by dry westerly winds, the land —mostly covered then by grasses that had taken hold in a thin layer of topsoil—was broken open by frost in winter and baked till cracked in summer. Sudden, torrential rains pelted and cut the soft, broken rocks. Swollen by these storms, rivers similar to those that once had constructed the rocks began to erode them, cleaving gullies through the weakest rocks, and deepening and broadening ravines. In the swift course of their work, a network of waterways left behind rock pinnacles, battlements, escarpments and the other unique land forms shown on these pages.

Within a few more million years —granted a fairly constant climate— all the dramatic architecture of the Badlands will be scoured away, worn down to the shale that underlies the region. But all the while, a thin layer of soil will provide a hospitable environment for the grassy plants and flowers that will stretch across the horizon. The Badlands will have been only a scene of fascinating destruction that flickered through the earth's geological drama.

The physical history of the Badlands is revealed in its striated beauty. Each of the colored bands shown here is made up of a different rock: mudstone laid down during dry times appears as dark bands; siltstone, the product of wetter eras, is light.

Under a still, hot June sky, the White
River lies like a glistening film on
its bed. During dry periods when
the river is sluggish, as here, sediments
abraded from upstream rocks drop
down through the water to settle on
the bottom. But during cloudbursts, the.
swollen river rages through its
valley to sweep away the sediments
and tear into the banks on both sides.

Not yet scoured by erosion, this plain supports a rich grassland.

The Stubborn Cycle of Grass to Grass

A microcosm of the stages of Badlands erosion is captured in these photographs. Briefly established as a lush, rolling upland *(left above)*, the Badlands are vulnerable to the runoff of early summer rains. The water tears through the shallow-rooted grasses, carving out gullies, which soon become gorges.

These natural wedges grow rapidly—a river can deepen its runoff channel by a foot in only two years. And as the slopes become steeper *(left below)*, the grasses lose their precarious rootholds.

Patchy remnants of the protective blanket of grass and soil are now exposed to wind, sun and frost. While the weather works its cycle of wear, rain waters continue to rip at the soft, exposed rock layers, creating badlands. But even then seeds have sprouted in loose sediments on the valley bottoms, and in the midst of such devastation, there is a natural return to grassland.

The slopes of a ravine sliced by runoff water still provide a tenuous foothold for vegetation. Clumps of grasses, growing together to conserve moisture and share a root system, are the only greenery that can survive in a landscape that was once a gentle plain.

Beyond the sheer silt and clay flanks of an eroded Badlands gully lies a curious series of sod-covered terraces. A legacy of the increased precipitation during the ice age, these terraces resulted as engorged rivers dropped their rich sediments in the valley.

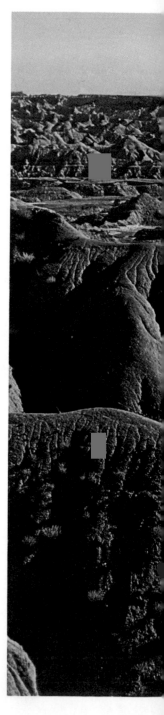

Sheep Mountain Table, where wild Audubon bighorns used to graze, was once an extensive upland prairie. It continues to shrink each year from the inroads of small streams eating away its flanks. Filled with abrasive rocks and clay dug from the slopes, the streams have already cut almost entirely through Sheep Mountain Table in one spot (upper left center). And in another geological eyeblink, these waters will reduce the mesa to nothing.

The Startling Shapes of Eroded Rock

There is almost no end to the variety of shapes assumed by the compliant land as it submits to water's erosive forces.

At right, layers of light-colored rock permeated with volcanic ash weather and erode into furrowed, pinnacled ridges, separated by deep ravines. At left, mudstone and siltstone fall away to expose the vertical edges of thin rock layers, called dikes, that slice across stretches of worn terrain. Dikes begin to form in crevices in rock strata when clay and silt are washed or blown into the fissures. Then these particles are cemented into a solid mass by mineral-bearing waters, so that the dikes often become harder than the surrounding rocks. As the softer, embracing rock face wears away, the dikes jut from the surface.

On the following pages is a dramatic gallery of other rock forms that occur as the Badlands respond to the frontal attacks—and subtle underminings—of erosive forces.

Vertical dikes stand out conspicuously (left) from the horizontal grain of their surrounding rock layers. Generally more resistant to erosion than are the softer rocks, the dikes remain in place as water wears away the rest.

Muddy columns standing together like organ pipes (right) are one of the varied patterns that result from water working on vertical cracks in volcanic ash. Here, the ravines between each fluted ridge are cut by tributaries running down to the White River.

Domed mounds called haystacks form in rock layers that are largely composed of clay. When the absorbent rock is doused by brief

rains, moisture lodges in the upper layers. Gravity draws the soaked clay over the dry interior, forcing the rock into a haystack shape.

Under a wind-whipped pinnacle that dominates a barren lowland, chunks of channel sandstone slowly topple as their bases disintegrate.

Rainwash that gnawed clay from beneath a sandstone stratum left these odd mushroom shapes.

This cave mouth was scooped from rock by water swirling down from a crack in the cliff above.

Beneath stagnant cloud layers of a June day, a desolate sweep of Badlands lies barren and vulnerable. Yet within this realm of aridity and

eroded rock, in the deep depression, or slump, at the lower right, enough soil and moisture have been trapped to support some greenery.

3/ Thunderhorse and Other Relics

*...For all around us at the base of these walls
and pyramids were heads and tails, and fragments of
the same, of species which are not known
to exist at the present day.*   DR. FERDINAND V. HAYDEN/ 1855

As Sage Creek twists through the northwest corner of Badlands National Monument on its way to the Cheyenne River about 10 miles away, the watercourse can be treacherous. By early summer the stream is running low, only a few inches deep in most places, and the sandy, pebbly bottom appears to offer solid footing. But at intervals there are patches of sucking gumbo in which an unwary hiker can sink over his ankles. On one walk down the Sage Creek stream bed I learned this the hard way by losing a low, buckled boot; I had to walk out with one stocking foot, and I was cautious on later excursions. Wherever I could, I used stepping stones.

And so, on a scorching afternoon in late June, I stepped onto what seemed to be a slightly round-backed oval rock about two feet long. It was slick and I slipped off, sinking deep into the surrounding mud. But as I struggled out, I noticed an unmistakable pattern on the rock where my sliding boot had wiped away a thin coating of clay. I scooped water from the shallows, quickly washed the rock clean—and there, perfect in every detail, was a fossilized turtle shell.

Only a couple of weeks before I had seen a large turtle, alive and behaving as briskly as turtles can manage, on a mudflat beside the White River. Lord knows what its dim thoughts were, where it was going or whence it came. In general appearance it was very much like my fossil stepping stone, but tens of millions of years had passed between the death of the one and the life of the other. I stood still in the stream bed, feeling the dry west wind on my cheek and musing about the enduring nature of such species.

Turtle shells are among the most common of the hundreds of varieties of animal fossils to be found in the Badlands. Most are smaller than mine, although near the Black Hills, in a section of Pierre shale, a 12-foot-long giant was once dug up. The individual plates of the shells are in most cases separated or broken, so that fossil turtles often resemble little heaps of prehistoric Indian potsherds. Although my creature's shell was complete, it did not have its head and tail—but then, most turtle fossils don't. The ligaments decompose quickly after the animal dies, and the parts that they connected fall off and are lost before they can become fossilized. But I didn't care about the missing parts; it was the reach of time that awed me. The animal whose stony remains I had slipped on had lived during the Oligocene epoch—from 25 to 40 million years ago.

The Oligocene lasted only about 15 million years, merely an eyeblink in geologic terms, but it was a particularly fascinating epoch, midway between the end of the age of dinosaurs and the age of man. The huge and the ferocious reptiles had all departed, leaving behind only smaller representatives of their kind, including my turtle. Man had not yet reared his head. Without either *Tyrannosaurus rex* or *Homo sapiens*, the world got along well enough. This was especially true in the region now known as the Badlands. In those days, the region was home to a huge variety of mammals, including the ancestors of the horse and the camel, a giant, ill-tempered pig, and a savage sabertooth cat—one of the most formidable killers ever to walk the earth. Largest of the Badlands mammals during the Oligocene was the titanothere, a monster that vaguely resembled a rhinoceros, standing eight feet tall at the shoulder and weighing up to five tons. Petrified titanothere bones were discovered by Indians in the Badlands; they gave the beast a name —Thunderhorse. They also created legends about it. According to one story, the giant horse sometimes returned to earth during thunderstorms to kill buffalo. A variation on this theme had Thunderhorse driving a buffalo herd conveniently close to a camp of Sioux who were on the verge of starvation, thus assuring them survival.

Thunderhorse did not survive through the end of the Oligocene; a cooling climate changed the nature of its food supply, and it could not adapt. But at the beginning of the Oligocene, conditions for the titanothere—and its companion host of other animals—were extremely hospitable. At that period, the Badlands wilderness was a low-lying plain with a warm, moist climate like that of present-day Florida. The broad Red River meandered across it, depositing debris scoured from the Black Hills. There were marshes and mudflats, and also drier areas of grassland and forest. In this abundance of water and vegetation, animals thrived, evolved for several million years—then fell upon hard times. Some died out, some migrated, and some managed to adapt and survive where they were.

The cause of the hard times—and the stimulus that led to selective survival—was the development of a polar air mass that displaced and disrupted the previous circulation of mild air. In the particular case of the Badlands, there was another, later factor of climatic change. Westerly winds blowing from the Pacific Ocean were forced ever higher by the continuing uplift of many parts of the Rocky Mountains. The winds became cooler and, as their moisture condensed, drier. As they blew across the Badlands they inexorably dehydrated the humid floodplain. The process of climatic change took an enormous length of time—millions upon millions of years—during which the rivers continued to deposit their sediments on the plain in ever-deepening layers, burying the remains of countless animals. The fossils that lie strewn across the Badlands today are an enduring record of Oligocene life—the greatest such fossil deposit in the world.

The process of fossilization is not a very complicated one, but it requires just the right conditions. These conditions were approximated, I suspect, when I lost my boot in the gumbo of Sage Creek. Rapid burial is the secret. The mud suddenly engulfed the shoe; conceivably, in a million years, the mud, having turned to rock and the rock having eroded away, will yield up my boot again—petrified, a wonder to science. An animal's remains may be preserved if they are quickly plunged into an environment, such as muck, where oxygen cannot get at them and promote rapid decomposition. If the remains stay buried for a long period and if the mud slowly hardens, ground water may seep into the tiny spaces within the animal bones, depositing silica, calcium carbonate or other minerals; the bones are thus fossilized.

The term fossil—from the Latin *fossilis*, meaning dug up—applies to any trace of a prehistoric organism. It can be the delicate imprint of a fern or an insect's wing, a lizard's petrified excrement, a fly preserved in amber, a seed or a mammoth frozen in ice. But in the Badlands, most fossils, at least those evident to the casual observer, are bones. Or-

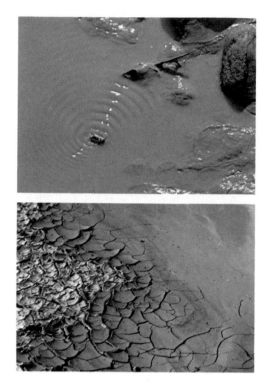

The making of a potential fossil begins at top, as a fly is trapped in a muddy pool. After death, the corpse sinks into the drying mud (bottom). In time, the mud may harden into rock, while the fly's body decomposes and leaves a fossil cast of the creature.

dinarily, only the hard parts of an animal—shell, tooth, bone, hoof, horn, beak—are preserved in this manner. Usually, they are disconnected and it is exceptional for a complete skeleton to be found.

Conditions for the fossilization of animals in the Oligocene Badlands, in the marshes and mudflats and steadily thickening layers of sediment, were ideal. The layers of sediment, which were laid down very rapidly, have never been disturbed by earthquakes or other violent actions of the earth. As erosion has cut the layers away, they have revealed their contents in neat chronological order.

Many of the animals whose fossils are found in the Badlands seem familiar enough—mice, squirrels, beavers and rabbits. They are not precisely similar to their modern descendants, but the likeness is sufficient. However, I find it very difficult to resist the fascination of such awesome and grotesque-looking beasts as the titanothere, which had twin hornlike protuberances, blunt at the tips, that rose from its snout and projected left and right like the arms of a V. Horns and heft well equipped a titanothere to fight off its foes, although older and weaker titanotheres were often killed by another fearsome creature—the lupine *Hyaenodon horridus*, a bear-sized carnivore with huge fangs.

The titanothere had a thick skin and a thicker skull. And though the heads of large individuals were three feet long, their brains were only about the size of a man's clenched fist. However, it was not stupidity that killed off the beast, but a classic case of inability to cope with a changing environment—the cause of most animal extinctions. The titanothere was a browser; its teeth, including four-inch-square molars, were ideal for grinding the soft forest vegetation that covered the Badlands early in the Oligocene. But these back teeth were low-crowned and incapable of grinding tougher matter. By the middle of the epoch, as the climate slowly turned cooler and drier, the titanothere could not adapt to grazing the new, more rugged grasses that were replacing its old fodder. Probably it starved into extinction, although there are several other theories of the animal's demise, including the effect of new diseases spread by insects such as tsetse flies. Whatever the cause, the titanothere vanished, leaving a plentiful record of fossils but no descendants in today's world.

Thunderhorse fossils are relatively rare, but a large number of fossils of all sorts of other creatures can be found in the anthills of the Badlands. In excavating their underground homes, the harvester ants of the Badlands pile the debris—grains of sand, pebbles and anything else they find below the surface—in conical mounds around the entrances to their nests. Since the ants can't tell a pebble from a fossil, they often pick up tiny bones and teeth of rodents and other small Oligocene animals as well as broken fragments of larger creatures. Indeed, in 1965 one fossil-hunting expedition found about 5,000 specimens, including traces of more than 25 kinds of fish, amphibians, reptiles and mammals, in some 100 anthills south of the Great Wall.

I have spent hours grubbing through anthills in search of these minute but fascinating fossils, and have always been able to come up with enough to fill the palm of my hand. (The only problem, and it does become irritating, is that one also picks up ants, and ants bite.) My finds have included fragments of the teeth of animals called oreodonts, among the most common inhabitants of the Badlands during the Oligocene. Oreodonts—from Greek words meaning mountain and tooth —existed in at least 22 varieties, ranging from the size of opossums to that of sheep. They once wandered in herds across Wyoming, Colorado, the Dakotas, Montana and Nebraska, and for a long time—from 45 million to about three million years ago—they adapted to all sorts of environments. Some oreodonts climbed trees; others spent much time in the water. They had piglike bodies and long, skinny, ratlike tails, and they chewed cuds like cows. But for all their versatility they disappeared like the titanothere, and no relatives survive.

In addition to searching in anthills, I have learned to look for fossils where rock fragments have recently fallen down a cliff or slope, exposing new surfaces. But often, rather than hunting for fossil bones directly, I look for a clue that will tell me whether I'm likely to find anything worthwhile nearby. One of the best hints is the presence among the rocks of the fossilized seeds of the hackberry tree. In the Oligocene, the hackberry dotted the Badlands landscape. Its seed fossils, preserved just like tiny bones, are about the size of BB shot, and white. They contrast nicely with the fawn-colored earth, and thus are easy to spot. I have found hundreds of hackberry seed fossils without much trouble. As a rule, animal fossils were not far away, perhaps because the trees thrived in or near muddy areas where creatures were trapped.

Because of the remoteness of the Badlands, their fossil treasures did not attract much attention until about 130 years ago. The early French-Canadian trappers who passed through the region were pragmatic men, concerned with the pelts of live animals and not the bones of dead ones. The first serious fossil collecting in the Badlands was begun by an amateur who made his living in the fur trade: Alexander Culbertson, chief agent of the American Fur Company on the upper Missouri. By 1843, Culbertson, a Pennsylvanian, had developed strong ties to this region. He had married Na-ta-wis-ta-cha (Medicine Snake Woman), the attractive 15-year-old daughter of a Blackfoot chief, and thus enjoyed the respect of the Indians. He also had a scientific bent. For two years during the 1840s, Culbertson dug up a variety of fossils in the Badlands, including a fragment of the lower jaw of a titanothere and another fragment of a creature once believed to be the camel's ancestor. Eventually, part of Culbertson's collection was presented to the prestigious Academy of Natural Sciences of Philadelphia and interest in exploring the Badlands quickened.

Culbertson's finds were soon overshadowed by those unearthed by John Evans, a government geologist, on an expedition in 1849. Among the fossils Evans turned up were an 18-foot-long titanothere skeleton and a one-ton turtle. The appearance of many other fossils astonished Evans. They were, he noted, in "such a perfect condition and present so fresh an appearance, that the light is reflected back from the enameled surface of the teeth with as much brilliancy as from highly polished steel. Were it not for their ponderous character, and their strange physiognomy, one might well suppose them to be the bones of recent animals, which had been bleached but for a season." Despite his joy of discovery, Evans was almost undone by the Badlands' scorching summer weather, reporting that it was "unmitigated by a breath of air or the shelter of a solitary shrub."

In 1853, Evans ran into something that irritated him even more—the threat of competition—while he was planning another visit to the Badlands with a geologist named Benjamin Shumard. By now he felt that he had prior rights to fossil hunting in the area, and when he learned that another expedition was forming—inspired, ironically, by his own report on his 1849 trip—he violently opposed it. One of the two members of the rival team was 23-year-old Ferdinand Hayden, a physician who was working as a geologist for the U.S. Geological and Geographical Survey of the Territories; his collaborator was an older man, a self-taught paleontologist named Fielding Meek. Hayden and Meek, having pored over Evans' survey of the Badlands, received private sponsorship for a collecting trip to the Dakota country. Feelings between the rivals ran so high that ultimately two mediators of impeccable standing in the scientific community were called in: Dr. George Engelmann, the pioneer botanist, and the eminent naturalist Professor Jean Louis Agassiz of Harvard. After they had pointed out the obvious—that the Badlands

A fossil turtle, perhaps as old as 35 million years, lies partly broken on a Badlands slope. Through the millennia the fossil was encased in hardened clay or rock, which preserved the clearly etched pattern of the animal's original shell. Once the casing has been eroded away, however, such fossils, exposed to the weather, last only about seven years. This specimen is already almost half destroyed.

contained enough fossils for everyone—both parties got underway.

For Evans and Shumard, this Badlands visit turned out to be only a stopover; a new government assignment sent them on to Oregon to help on an Army survey of a transcontinental rail route. The adventures of Hayden and Meek began aboard the Missouri River steamer that was taking them toward the Badlands. One of their fellow passengers was an Indian agent, whose baggage included some $8,000 worth of supplies—beans, flour, kegs of powder and shot—to placate any restive Sioux in the Badlands. It then occurred to the fossil hunters that unfriendly Indians might turn out to cause at least as much unpleasantness as rival fossil-hunting parties. Hayden and Meek enlisted the agent's help. As Meek reported it, the agent agreed to tell the Sioux that "the Great Father has given us leave to travel in their country, and if they steal our horses or give us any trouble he will send them no more presents."

Thus reassured, Hayden and Meek spent three undisturbed weeks in the Badlands amassing a large and valuable collection of mammalian remains. The experience was so tantalizing that Hayden returned for several more forays in the next few decades. On one occasion, traveling alone and wearing a business suit, he crossed paths with some Indians, and a few tense moments followed until they discovered that all he had with him was a pick and a sack of rocks. Deciding that he was insane, and hewing to their tradition of not harming the mentally ill, they left him alone, dubbing him Man Who Picks Up Rocks Running.

At times the Indians proved less tolerant of fossil hunters. In 1874, after General George Custer reported the finding of gold in the Black Hills, the Sioux became particularly disgruntled at the prospect of hordes of white men overrunning their land. That year no less august a personage than Othniel Marsh, president of the National Academy of Sciences, decided to visit the area. Accompanied by an Army escort and traveling after dark, he slipped past Indian lookouts and entered the Badlands through the Red Cloud Agency on the banks of the White River. He hurried out only two days later, however, when he heard that a Sioux war party was searching for the Big Bone Chief.

That was the only time Marsh himself ventured into the Badlands, but over the years the assistants he employed in his capacity as professor of paleontology at Yale dug up thousands of fossils, most notably providing evidence of the evolution of the horse—one of the few animals that managed to evolve from pre-Oligocene times to the present.

The forebears of the horse—*Hyracotherium*, also known as *Eohip-*

A six-inch-wide fossil mollusk called an ammonite lies partly locked in a matrix of shale, a solidification of the sea mud in whose embrace the snail died. The ammonite, which resembles the chambered nautilus, flourished in the ocean that covered the Badlands more than 70 million years ago.

pus, or dawn horse—first appeared on earth some 15 million years before the Oligocene. A forest dweller about the size of a fox terrier, *Eohippus* had four toes on its front feet and three in back. By the Oligocene, the horse in the Badlands was as large as a collie, with three toes on its splayed front and hind feet to help it maneuver both in the forests and swampy plains. *Mesohippus,* as the Oligocene horse is called, was one of the most numerous creatures in the Badlands. It was still a browser, with low-crowned teeth suitable for chewing soft leaves, but its brain had become larger and its legs more slender than those of its ancestors. As the forests and wetlands of the Oligocene gave way to drier plains, *Mesohippus* evolved into a highly specialized animal that began to resemble the modern horse. Its molars became longer, developing high crowns capable of tearing up the new, tougher plains grasses. And its legs grew longer in proportion to the rest of its body; its side toes diminished in size and it developed a single, central toe with a hoof, which increased speed and agility on smooth ground.

After the Oligocene, the horse migrated from its various habitats in the American West across land bridges to every continent except Australia. About 8,000 years ago, for reasons not yet understood, the horse became extinct in North America, and did not return until the gold-seeking Spanish conquistadors of the 16th Century brought it with them in their galleons.

One morning, from my camp on Sheep Mountain Table, I looked down through the early mist at a lone horse grazing in a distant valley and thought about its extraordinary history. The animal seemed perfectly at home where it was, yet its kind had taken a fantastic journey in time and space. It had walked from that valley north to Alaska, across the Bering Strait, across Asia, across much of Europe and south to Spain. There it had taken ship for Mexico, whence it had walked north—back to the place where it had originated.

Scientists were not always ready to accept this story of remarkable wanderings. Until 1876, they believed that the modern genus of horse, *Equus,* had originated in Asia or Europe. But in that year England's Thomas Huxley, the earliest defender of Darwin's theory of evolution, arrived in the United States for a series of lectures. Othniel Marsh invited Huxley to Yale and showed him a collection of horse fossils, including some of *Mesohippus,* from the Badlands. This convinced Huxley that the horse had, in fact, evolved in North America; there was no evidence of an Oligocene horse anywhere in Europe.

Today horse fossils are fairly common in the Badlands, although they have escaped me during my expeditions. Nor have I been able to come up with any fossils of another beast—the camel—that, like the horse, underwent most of its evolution in North America. At the dawn of the Oligocene the camel had no hump and was the size of a sheep. During the Oligocene it grew as large as a gazelle, and later it, too, walked across land bridges to Asia, Europe and South America. It came back to its ancestral home in the last century under unfortunate circumstances. In 1856, Jefferson Davis, then U.S. Secretary of War, imported 34 camels from Egypt and elsewhere to transport Army supplies across the deserts of the Southwest. A camel can carry as much as 1,000 pounds, but it is notoriously stubborn and obstreperous, and it did not get along well with American bullwhackers and mule skinners. Furthermore, they were unable to learn the knack of packing a camel so that its load wouldn't fall off. Even worse, the camel stank, and the odor caused horses, oxen and mules to stampede. After a few years the camels were turned loose, and white and Indian hunters wiped them out.

During the camel's prehistoric life in North America, one of its predators was the sabertooth cat. About the size of a leopard, but more heavily built, the sabertooth's deadly pair of three-inch-long fangs curved down from its upper jaw. The lower jaw was hinged so that it could open to a 90° angle while the cat sliced and stabbed its prey. In a kill, the sabertooth would leap on its victim, dig in with its claws, and then strike down with its fangs.

Evidence of the sabertooth's ferocity survives at the museum of the South Dakota School of Mines and Technology in the form of a skull of another Oligocene cat, called *Dinictis*, which was almost as large as the sabertooth but lacked its dental armament. In the left-front region of the skull is an enormous wound, almost certainly inflicted by a sabertooth. The sabers did not penetrate the brain, however, and the wound partly healed while the victim lived on for a while.

Other beasts of the ancient Badlands were both fascinating and formidable. I have examined the skull of one, a 10-foot-long entelodont, or giant pig, that appeared to be an even more gruesome brute than the sabertooth. An entelodont skull—fully three feet long—is the prize of Max Hauk, an amateur fossil collector in the town of Wall. Over the years Max has gathered up hundreds of fossils in the Badlands area outside the monument, including traces of sabertooths. But it is plain from his collection that no prehistoric beast of the area compared with the entelodont. Standing six feet tall, with a humped back, the entelodont carried an array of teeth that look as if they could have demolished anything on the landscape, although the creature apparently existed on roots. It was evidently also as ugly in disposition as in appearance, and frequently attacked even fellow entelodonts. The entelodont's fate was the same as that of the titanothere. It could not adapt to changes in climate and vegetation, and perished.

Like titanothere remains, entelodont fossils are relatively rare finds. In general, however, Badlands fossils are easy enough to come upon, although one can make an occasional small error. One summer day—the temperature was 100° F.—I was out hunting with Max Hauk somewhere north of Badlands National Monument. While Max was preoccupied with his own investigations I spotted a curious shape near the base of a slope. It was plate sized, hard as a rock and heavy enough to be a fossil. Triumphantly I took it back to Max for identification. He took one look at it and somehow refrained from laughing. "That," he said, "is cow dung." Then, seeing the wounded look on my face, Max added graciously, "It petrifies fast."

But there can be triumphs too. On another occasion Max and his wife, Nancy, and I were prowling near Cottonwood Creek when I stumbled over an elongated rust-colored object and *knew* I had found an important fossil. I called Max, and he immediately identified it as the leg bone of a titanothere. I was tremendously excited. I had been proud of my fossil turtle back in Sage Creek, but a turtle is a turtle and a titanothere is a Thunderhorse. Only about 30 inches of the titanothere bone were exposed; the ends were buried in hard clay. There was no way for us to excavate the fossil; nor could we tell what other parts of the creature might still have been concealed. We stayed there staring at the bone for some time, and I tried to imagine what this spot had looked like some 35 or 40 million years ago when the titanothere was alive. Then we walked away. But I think about returning one day and carefully digging deeper, and perhaps unearthing an entire skeleton. I even daydream that my find might be recognized as a new breed of titanothere and be named *Titanotherium clarki.* That is worth thinking—and daydreaming—about.

NATURE WALK / # Up Coyote Creek

PHOTOGRAPHS BY DAVID CAVAGNARO

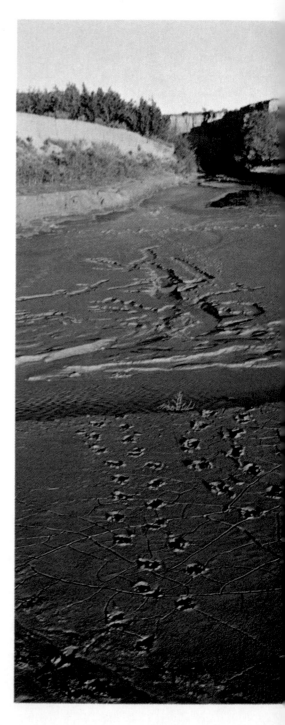

Entering South Dakota from Nebraska, the White River snakes along on a leisurely but erratic course. At a point seven miles west of the dusty little Badlands town of Interior, the river suddenly turns south for two miles, then doubles back. In the crook of that deep riverbed, a small spring-fed stream named Coyote Creek enters the White. At that remote confluence on the Pine Ridge Reservation of the Oglala Sioux, five of us gathered shortly after dawn on a shimmering mid-May morning, having forded the river while it was still roiling from an overnight storm.

For several minutes, all five men —photographer David Cavagnaro; botanist Theodore Van Bruggen of the University of South Dakota at Vermillion; Max Hauk, a self-taught naturalist from Wall, South Dakota; Lane Johnston, local rancher and the owner of this 700-acre tract; and I —stood silent, caught in the spell of the place's wild yet serene splendor. Ankle deep in the mud flats at the mouth of Coyote Creek, we faced up the little stream. To our left and 150 feet above us, a long swath of green was barely visible. This lofty oasis, paradoxically called a slump, was our destination for the day. One of the largest of its kind in the Bad-

lands, the elevated green enclave was produced in prehistoric times when the river, its channel much higher than today, had undercut its bank. The erosion caused a rockfall that formed a basin for water where plants and animals could thrive.

We moved slowly along the mud flats up Coyote Creek. Despite the rain of a few hours before, a thin earthen crust had formed and already was beginning to bake and crack. Frozen in the crust, leading to and from the narrow stream, were the tracks of a porcupine, that clumsy creature whose small imprints at a distance bear remarkable resemblance to those of another awkward animal: man. As we walked we saw, within a few hundred yards of one another, the tracks of a deer, a rabbit and a pair of coyotes with four pups. All had obviously sought Coyote Creek's sweet water, which animals much prefer to the acrid, silty water of the White River.

My attention was distracted by the flitting of a spring-azure butterfly, and to follow it, I pushed through a thicket on the bank. When I emerged after a hopeless pursuit, Max Hauk grinned. "Looks to me," he kidded, "like you're trying to walk away with some of our famous flora."

I discovered that my pants legs were liberally studded with burs (in removing them, I counted 57). They were the fruit of the common cocklebur, a plant with few redeeming features. In its seedling stage the leaves are extremely poisonous if

COCKLEBUR SEEDS

eaten by animals, causing nausea, labored breathing and a wobbly gait. Although toxicity decreases as the cocklebur grows older, the plant develops a taste so bitter that most animals avoid it. Yet for all this, it may be admired. Each spiny fruit encases two seeds that can endure for as long as eight years before germinating. Meanwhile, the burs are distributed far and wide by animals and birds (and pants legs) to which they have attached themselves.

MOUTH OF COYOTE CREEK

CLIFF-SWALLOW NESTS

BEE BURROWS

HALF-BURIED BUFFALO BONES

Of all the areas of the Badlands, this is among the most fecund in animal life and verdant in plants. Yet even here we found constant reminders of death and destruction. The creek banks soon steepened to near-vertical heights of 30 feet or more. Midway on one of these faces, we saw the ruins of several cliff-swallow nests. The individual dabs of clay that the hard-working birds had painstakingly plastered together were, for the most part, still in place. But we noticed that these were old nests; the mouths of some gaped wide, torn away either by the elements or by predator birds. And though cliff swallows were swarming throughout the Badlands, they had not returned to repair and reinhabit these now-forlorn nests.

Nearby, the cliff face was marked by scores of small holes, originally drilled by a species of solitary bee (as opposed to the hiving bee) whose females had provisioned minuscule burrows with pollen balls for their larvae to feed upon. But birds hungry for the larvae, had pecked away at the burrows and enlarged them. Now the bee burrows, like the cliff-swallow nests, were empty.

Protruding from an opposite bank, we saw some buffalo bones, deeply buried but as yet far from fossilized. These remains, whose age we could not determine because the strata yielded too few clues, gave silent evidence of the herds of beasts—ancestors or relations of this buffalo —that had thundered across this prairie by the millions until gunned nearly to extinction a century ago.

COTTONWOOD ALONG COYOTE CREEK

A bit farther upstream, the steep banks gave way to grassy floodplains, populated by stately cottonwood trees, two of them so close together that their trunks appeared to rise from the same roots. On the ground beneath their outstretched branches lay the slowly disintegrating debris of still another aged cottonwood tree, naked and dead.

Predators and Prey

Not far away, at the foot of a younger cottonwood, rested a mass of quills held loosely together by dried skin tissue. It was a decomposed porcupine, completely gutted, with no traces of flesh and only a few bones. Although the porcupine is the least aggressive of animals, this spiny creature, as many a larger, more ferocious predator has learned to its anguish, is formidably armed for its own defense. It is born with some 30,000 soft quills, which harden within a half-hour of emergence from the womb. But the porcupine's underbelly remains unprotected throughout its life, a fact of which that fearless little killer the bobcat is well aware.

Coincidentally, Max Hauk had recently spotted a bobcat prowling these very premises. "It was," he recalled, "the biggest I've seen in more than 40 years in the Badlands." Lane Johnston went on to explain how this porcupine had probably died. "The porcupines go up a tree and out on a branch to get away. But the cats swing out on a lower branch and swipe at their guts. Those cats are active. Oh man, they are active."

As the morning lengthened, the air

IN LOGSTON SPRING MARSH

ELM BARK CHEWED BY PORCUPINE

grew still and sultry. High, scattered cloud puffs cast occasional shadows upon us while we waded up Coyote Creek. Cottonwood gave way to aspen, peach-leafed willow, hackberry, red osier dogwood and that tree so familiar to Easterners, the American elm, dwarfed here but still unmistakable. Dense thickets of chokecherry, buffaloberry and wild plum offered impenetrable barriers to any of us wishing to stray from the creek's course. Water weeds appeared in the bed of the stream. We were nearing the point, about a meandering mile south of the White River confluence, where the waters fed by Logston Spring trickle into Coyote Creek. And soon we turned west into the spring's marshes—actually a series of small, grass-tufted islands where the hollows between the hummocks

have become inundated with water.

Ted Van Bruggen, an enthusiast in his calling, was elated, splashing shin deep to collect plant specimens. "I'll bet you never thought you'd find anything like *this* in the Badlands," he told me. Giant bulrushes with tubular stems, through which the plants feed their submerged roots, vied for space with water parsnip and matted green islands of beggar's-tick—named because the barbs of its fruit stick to animals' fur.

Near the edges of the marshes, the American elm was dominant. But many of the trees were dying; our friend the porcupine had been at work. Although the porcupine will eat just about any vegetation, trees seem a particular favorite. Porcupines are excellent climbers and it is no trick at all for them to reach mid-

trunk of an appetizing tree. Using large, chisel-like teeth, they strip away the outer bark in search of the starches and sugars stored in the inner bark. Porcupines have been known to stay in a single tree for as long as a week, gnawing away until the trunk is completely girdled. Unfortunately, this kills the tree.

Logston Spring, as we soon discovered, is not one spring but many, scattered over a considerable area. The springs are the result of ground water that has seeped down through the Badlands clay until reaching the impermeable shale that at one time formed the floor of an inland sea. Water trapped there inevitably exerts pressure to escape; in the Logston Spring area, wind and rain have provided the route—erosion has eaten away the junctures between clay and shale. Some of the springs emerge as mere oozes on soft slopes; others cascade as miniature waterfalls down steep banks.

The sweet, clean waters of Logston Spring afford a bounty to plant and wildlife—and a wilderness delight for humans. At the western head of the marshes, the dominant water plant is a handsome little sedge *Carex haydenii,* named after F. V. Hayden, a devoted plant collector as well as a pioneer Badlands fossil hunter. The sedge's stalk is crowned by a long cluster of orange-yellow male flowers above two more modestly hued female spikes, which receive the falling pollen.

Most numerous among the marshes' animal denizens are frogs. Near a *Carex* cluster on a blanched, half-submerged branch, a leopard frog perched, unperturbed by our noisy approach. An athlete of the marshlands, this frog can cover six feet in a single bound. However, its voice sounds lazy and halfhearted to me, more like the sound of creaking sad-

CAREX SEDGE

CASCADE IN THE MARSH

dle leather than a throaty croak.

As we looped back toward Coyote Creek along the southern edges of the marsh chain, David Cavagnaro, who has eyes as sharp as his camera lenses, spotted a red-winged blackbird nest hidden within a wild-plum thicket. Shaped in a perfect circle and fashioned from intertwined marsh sedges, the nest contained a single egg, pale blue with faint blotches. As David was photographing the nest, Max Hauk suddenly remarked, "That ole girl up there doesn't like us." Sure enough, from the top of a cedar a female redwing glowered down upon us with obvious anxiety and disapproval. We departed quietly, and the expectant mother bird fluttered down to her precious nest.

Climbing the Gumbo

Crossing Coyote Creek, our group walked east across a patch of prairie with mixed grasses and paused to draw breath before starting the climb toward the slump. The time was midafternoon, the temperature

LEOPARD FROG

RED-WINGED BLACKBIRD NEST

BASE OF GUMBO SLOPE

was in the 80s. To achieve the height of the mesa that overlooked the slump from the north, we faced a half-mile climb up a so-called gumbo slope, whose multitude of hummocks had been rounded and gullied by washoff. The basic material of the slope was ancient clay, deposited more than 30 million years ago by a now-extinct river that traversed the area. Crumbly and treacherous when dry, as it now was, gumbo is positively perilous when slick—and I was hardly cheered by the sight of dark clouds far to the west.

Hunting for Agates

Partway up the slope, we were met by Lane Johnston's wife, Midge, and Max Hauk's wife, Nancy, who had been hunting for rocks and petrified wood in the gullies. Although this area is rich in agates transported from the southern Black Hills by the ancient river, the women had found none that day. Neither did I.

In fact, the finding and identifying of rare rocks is not my strong point. When I asked Midge to identify one

that I considered especially attractive, I was told, "That's a leavitrite."

"Oh?" I brightened.

"Yes," she said. "Leavitrite where it is." And I did.

Eventually I came across several pieces of petrified wood, although nothing to match the two specimens, discovered by Midge, resting next to a prickly pear.

I was surprised to find that even on this bare slope there was life. A Great Plains toad and a sagebrush lizard sought shade together in a sandy declivity. Gumbo lilies, larger than any I had seen before, were in full waxy-white flower. Of the 10 North American species of sage common to South Dakota, Ted Van Bruggen found six within 200 square feet. Textile onions rose from a rock bed. I dug up a bulb and found its outer coat reticulated with veins. True to its name, the bulb looked like patterned fabric, but as I bit into it I tasted garlic, not onion.

For various perverse reasons, my favorite plant on the slope was an

TEXTILE ONION

unattractive demiparasite known by a most unattractive name: bastard toadflax (for the delicate-minded, it is *Comandra umbellata*). Although the bastard toadflax has some photosynthetic tissue and is thus not fully parasitical, nonetheless it has no roots and lives by attaching itself to the roots of other plants.

By 4 p.m., we had climbed to a

PETRIFIED WOOD AND PRICKLY PEAR

BASTARD TOADFLAX

point on the mesa just above the slump. Although the storm clouds had passed us to the north, the sky was hazy and the breeze was hot, bringing little relief. We descended into the slump and walked about 300 yards across it to a spot near the White River precipice.

There, we turned and looked back up toward the mesa. Immediately before us was a stretch of sand reed grass, perfectly at home in the loose sandy soil. Beyond, we could see two distinct steps in the ground level, presumably the result of separate rockfalls occurring millions of years apart. First the terrain sloped upward about 30 feet. Beyond that —although mostly concealed from our view by a cedar forest—was a lesser slope leading to the mesa top. We headed for the cedars.

The air in the grove was cool, the aromatic scent of the cedars was pleasant. As we began to walk eastward along a half mile of the slump, we were accompanied by the song of a western meadowlark. Poems have been written about the melody of the lark, and Tennyson actually translated its warbling as, "I'll never love any but you." However, the western meadowlark is actually a member of the blackbird family, and to me, its message, usually delivered at the top of its lungs, is, "Plant . . . your . . . wheat . . . right here." The bird apparently took a fancy to us, and its canary-colored breast flashed in and out of sight as it flew from tree to tree along our path.

While walking we encountered moments of excitement: a huge cot-

SAND REED GRASS ON SLUMP MOUNDS

tontail rabbit startled us all when it bounded among our legs and dived into its burrow. Midge Johnston and Nancy Hauk spotted a black-widow spider scuttling under a log; the creature seemed no more anxious to confront us than we it, and we gave the log a wide berth.

Life among the Cedars

Spring flowers were everywhere in bloom, blending their hues in the fragile white of Indian paintbrush, the blue and pink of penstemon. Ted Van Bruggen was still in his element, sometimes wriggling on his belly to get a closer look at the plants. It was thus that he encountered one of nature's more intriguing relationships: stick mound ants from a nearby colony were tending aphids on a clump of white sage. These ants are natively aggressive and they have a way, painful to humans and deadly to most other insects, of taking out their aggressions: first they bite; then they turn tail and spray a secretion of formic acid onto the wound. Aphids, on the other hand, are among the most helpless insects. They gorge themselves on plant juices, and the surplus liquid oozes from their bodies as a sweet substance known as honeydew.

Ants apparently find this nectar perfectly delicious. The ants "milk" the aphids by stroking them gently with their antennae, collecting tiny droplets from the ends of the aphids' abdomens. Although ants do not actually herd aphids, as has been reported, they do, in return for their honeydew, offer the aphids protection against other insects.

PENSTEMON

STICK MOUND ANTS TENDING APHIDS

INDIAN PAINTBRUSH

Failing to find such powerful protectors, some other Badlands insects ward off predators by their mere appearances. Such a one is the box elder bug, whose brilliant orange markings advertise a taste that birds apparently find thoroughly obnoxious. Once young birds discover the box elder's distastefulness, they file

BOX ELDER BUGS ON WALLFLOWER

away the memory of the gaudy coloration as reminder not to be tempted again. We found several of the showy but unappetizing creatures feeding on a western wallflower, where they were easy to spot against the pure yellow background. The bugs were perfectly safe, although our companion the western meadowlark—whose diet even includes the hairy caterpillars eschewed by most birds—flitted nearby.

No matter how fascinating its fauna and flora in any one place, the Badlands remain essentially badlands. And even within the cedar grove, where one might have thought the denser vegetation would have stabilized the soil, we found the ground rough and broken with gullies. In the slump, however, the gullies were thicket-filled; and thus

ly. Voracious eaters, they can defoliate a tree in short order.

Dusk was approaching as we neared the end of our trail through the cedar groves. And although no storm clouds were in sight, both Lane Johnston and Max Hauk, keen to the swiftness with which Badlands weather can change, agreed

utes, it flew down to feed on another dandelion, then returned to precisely the same spot on the tree. This process was repeated, and whenever other butterflies flew near the tree, the red admiral bristled its wings in what must have been a threat.

Interestingly, this insect turns to feeding on flowers only when there

RED-ADMIRAL BUTTERFLY

TENT CATERPILLARS

perhaps the erosive forces had been arrested—at least for a while.

As we picked our way through a tangle of chokecherry bushes we nearly pulled down several clouds of gossamer fabric strung between branches. These were the tentlike homes of moth larvae, and I recognized them as the eastern tent caterpillar. The filmy nets apparently serve this species as resting places between meals. When young, they feed on leaves blown by the wind or trapped within their tents, but when mature, the caterpillars forage wide-

that they smelled rain. It was time to go: we would have to ford the White River again, and that stream is nothing to trifle with during or after a storm. Still, we lingered for a few moments to watch the activities of a red-admiral butterfly, a beautiful creature with orange-red slashes bisecting its white-spotted brown forewings and fringing its smaller hind wings. When we first saw the butterfly, it was feeding contentedly on a dandelion. Then, apparently sated, it fluttered away to rest on the trunk of a cedar. After several min-

are many butterflies around. Otherwise, it seems to prefer rotting fruit or oozing sap. Clearly anticipating competition, our butterfly had staked out this spot and was exercising territorial rights.

We departed reluctantly, taking one last look from the slump, looking down upon the cedars and the White River to a grassland with Badlands buttes in the dim distance. It had been a good day in a good place. As we descended from the slump, the last thing we heard was the meadowlark bidding farewell.

FLOODPLAIN OF THE WHITE RIVER

4/ A Badlands Bestiary

It was the greatest game country that I ever saw.

CHARLES SACKETT, TRAPPER/ C. 1880

Like most people who have never seen the Badlands, I assumed before I went there that among the eroded wastes, in that harsh semiarid climate, I would be lucky to find any animal life beyond a few snakes and lizards. My mistake was to think of the Badlands as a desert, which they are not, rather than as a prairie, which they are. A rather fancifully carved-up prairie, maybe, but a true grassland for all that, populated with about every kind of animal life a grassland can support.

Even a casual traveler through Badlands National Monument would notice immediately that the place is full of birds and might not be surprised to learn that, counting migratory visitors as well as summer, winter and year-round residents, more than 120 different species have been sighted in the Badlands at one time or another. What might surprise the traveler, and certainly surprised me, is that the Badlands also offer 34 different mammals, all the way from nine varieties of mice to the biggest land animal in the New World, the bison. The reptiles I had expected to find in undisputed possession of the Badlands run a poor third. Even if you throw in the amphibians as a makeweight, the total comes to only seven species divided into 25 varieties, and a dozen of those are listed as "rare." Altogether, a formidable array of wildlife and as fascinating a menagerie as I have ever encountered, endlessly engaging whether they are making love, war or just a living.

A combination of these activities nourishes the annual hostilities of the Great Grackle-Swallow War. On the Pine Ridge Indian Reservation, about four miles south of Cedar Pass, the White River makes a sharp bend. On its southern bank it has scoured out a concave 80-foot-high bluff, plastered almost from top to bottom for 100 yards with hundreds of jug-shaped mud blisters. These are cliff-swallow nests.

The cliff swallow is a sturdy fellow only five to six inches long that flies more than 7,000 miles a year on its migrations between North and South America. Though the swallow's beak looks too short to be of any use in a fight, I saw one of these little birds harass a hawk one day, apparently just for the sport of it. The hawk, a female, had been soaring around her own nest, bothering nobody, but the swallow darted and pecked at her until the larger bird took refuge in altitude, climbing above her tiny tormentor's range. Another time, I decided to wade the river from the low north bank to the cliff to get a closer look at the colony; before I got halfway across I was swarmed by swallows. None actually touched me, but dozens darted within inches of my face—a distinctly uncomfortable feeling.

Yet the cliff swallows are not without natural enemies: every spring they must endure an unequal contest against flocks of grackles. The grackle—including the bronzed grackle, the variety found most frequently in the northern plains region—is an undeniably handsome bird about the size of a small crow, with iridescent head and neck hues of blending purples and greens. It is classed among the Oscines, a suborder of the songbird, and tries ceaselessly to live up to that billing. Its song, however, is a creaking squeak of maddening intensity that has been aptly compared to a wheelbarrow chorus. The grackle is a graceless flier and a ruthless ravager of eggs and nestlings of other birds.

For several weeks in May I watched with mounting tension a widening war between grackles and swallows. At this time of year the White River cliff swallows were in a full flurry of courtship and mating. For days they had been building new nests to replace those torn away by last winter's winds and rain, picking up in their beaks tiny pellets of mud and pasting them a dab at a time against the cliff face. The White River is an ideal source of supply; its banks are always wet with clay mud that sticks to anything and dries within minutes.

Each morning, usually beginning quite early, the swallows coursed like arrows up and down the river, some gathering mud, some hunting insects and some—like the couriers of a well-organized army—seeming to deliver dispatches to allied camps of other swallows. The morning the grackle raids began, however, the swallows, perhaps lulled by the balmy weather, did not appear until almost 8 o'clock. And when they did, they were in a state of extreme consternation. I soon spotted the cause of their concern. Perched on a mudbank across the river and looking every bit as sinister as Poe's raven was a female grackle. Behind and above her on a cottonwood branch and peering beady-eyed through the tree's wind-shaken leaves was a male grackle. The male seemed more than willing to let his mate do the dirty work. As he watched, she repeatedly hurtled across the river toward the swallows' nests, their eggs and their vulnerable young. And every time a swarm of swallows forced her back to the mudbank.

Day after day I watched the struggle develop. The first pair of grackles called in reinforcements until they numbered about 40. Small groups of them attacked here and there along the length and breadth of the swallow colony, as though probing for soft spots in the defense. After some days of this the grackles began mass attacks, flinging themselves in a body at one particular sector. The swallows adapted their routine to meet the challenge. They were out at dawn every day now and active until sunset. They still sent couriers up and down the river, but instead of foraging for mud or insects individually, they seemed to divide their duties. In watches apparently lasting about two hours each, some foraged, some patrolled the cliff face and the rest remained in their nests as a sort of ready reserve.

Despite these efforts, the grackles seemed to be winning. In about three weeks the grackles gobbled up all the eggs and chicks in a section of about 40 nests. Then the tide turned. While the swallows ignored the invaders as they flew to and from this area, they furiously repulsed all grackle attempts to expand the captured territory. And one morning, after a couple of weeks of this standoff, the grackles were gone. The swallows' remaining eggs had safely hatched and the young were on the wing, too large and resourceful to make easy prey for the grackles. The war was over.

Fortunately for me, the strain of covering the Great Grackle-Swallow War was relieved from time to time by incidents ranging from the less serious to the downright ridiculous, such as the vernal antics of the sharp-tailed grouse. Late one spring afternoon near Sage Creek, on a grassy two-acre knoll bordered by thickets, I heard a weird, resonant pigeon-like cooing that seemed to come from everywhere. Soon about 20 male grouse emerged from the brush and onto the knoll. They strutted about importantly, the purplish air sacs at the sides of their necks fully

Tense and alert to the photographer's threatening presence, these male pronghorns prepare to bolt—at speeds up to 60 miles an hour.

inflated as they continued to coo what I soon discovered was their mating call. For a while the males stood around as if wondering what to do next. Finally, one cock spread its wings, lowered its head nearly to ground level and made a mad dash across the knoll. Within seconds all the males were whirling and bowing, strutting and stamping their feet in a frenzy of sexual expectation. And then, apparently attracted by the commotion on the dancing ground, three females strolled onto the knoll. For a time they appeared to take not much notice of all the nonsense and walked unconcernedly about. But then they too became excited and drew near to the largest males, each of whom had described a kind of territory for himself, flapping and stamping noisily within its perimeter. As the boldest female approached, the largest male leaped on her back and they copulated quickly. Then another approached and the male mated again. In this way, all the females were eventually mated—but only with the biggest and flashiest of the male dancers. Many of the males continued to flap, exhausting themselves without ever attracting a female.

Among Badlands birds, the grouse is my favorite dancer. But the killdeer, a 10-inch-long bird, olive brown above and pure white below, gets my personal Avian Academy Award for acting. One June morning while crossing a meadow near Sage Creek, I inadvertently approached a killdeer nest hidden in a hollowed-out place in the grass. The result was dramatic. Shrieking "kill-dee, kill-dee," the female flapped and floundered and lurched drunkenly about, now dragging one wing along the ground as if it were broken, now dragging the other, occasionally beating both wings as though in an ecstasy of pain, and all the while getting farther and farther from the nest. The male meanwhile circled around, protesting my intrusion at the top of his lungs. Only after I had moved well away from the nest site did the show end.

In an even more theatrical encounter, I played straight man to the histrionics of the biggest ham in the whole class of reptiles—the hognose snake. It is known locally as a puff adder and behaves like a blend of Billy the Kid and Eleonora Duse. I came across one along the Cheyenne River and got an awful shock when it reared its head, spread its neck like a hooded cobra and, hissing hideously, coiled its nearly three-foot-long body for striking. Reminding myself that though the snake usually strikes when threatened, it rarely bites and is not venomous, I picked up a long stick and thrust it within range. The snake struck once, twice, thrice, four times, and then went into its big scene: it writhed all along its length, rolled over on its back, gave an agonized gasp and lay still, belly up, mouth open, tongue hanging out. I am told that at this point I could have tied the snake in a knot without getting the slightest reaction; if I had turned it over, it would quickly have flipped onto its back again to preserve the dead-snake image. I did not put the knowledge to the test; I merely applauded and left.

Most of the reptiles and amphibians of the Badlands are as harmless as the hognose snake, and though none is quite so entertaining, each has its points. The spadefoot toad, a comical-looking character with a toothed upper jaw, bulging catlike eyes and a stentorian voice, loves wet weather. During dry spells the toad retires to the nearest unoccupied gopher hole or makes its own retreat. Using the horny black edges of its hind feet, the creature can dig its way backward into loose soil so fast that it seems to melt out of sight. Equally retiring is the little blotched tiger salamander, known to Badlands natives as the mud puppy and regarded by some with loathing because of its slimy look and flat, blunt head. But as it paddles about drainage ditches and other dank places eating bugs and worms, it is less offensive than a flea.

The exception to the Badlands list of reputable reptiles is the prairie rattlesnake, smaller (up to about three feet in length), less poisonous and more timid than its relative, the western diamondback. Its bite can render a victim very ill; nevertheless, in the last 50 years there have been no recorded—I repeat, recorded—snake-bite fatalities in the Badlands. Those statistics are reassuring, but they do not mean that a person who gets bitten should not seek immediate medical attention.

As it turned out, I saw only two rattlers during my whole stay in the Badlands. One was winding its way across a back-country road I was driving down; as my vehicle overtook the snake, the car seemed to surge forward of its own volition. Although I had the feeling that the rattler had passed safely between the wheels, I did not go back to find out. The second rattlesnake was a baby less than a foot long, imprisoned alive in a glass jar and handed to me by a friend who knew I was interested in Badlands wildlife. He was right; I *was* interested—interested enough to have found out, for example, that though the venom glands are smaller, the bite of young rattlesnakes is as dangerous as that of their elders. I thanked my friend and handed back the jar unopened.

For that matter, I could have told him that, notwithstanding a certain heart-stopping fascination for the menace of the imprisoned viper, I am not preoccupied by the sensational aspects of the wilderness. Just as engrossing to me as the aggression of the grackles, the posturings of the sharp-tailed grouse and the tear-jerking performance of the hog-nose snake were the glimpses I got of Badlands animals simply going about their daily routines. Food gathering, of course, takes a good share of the waking hours of most of them. One of my favorite foragers is the grasshopper mouse, a short-legged six-inch-long rodent with a stubby tail and a keen carnivorous appetite. Emerging at dusk from its burrow, the mouse tracks down its prey—grasshoppers, scorpions, other mice—with the persistence of a coonhound, trotting along the trail nose to the ground in a very houndlike manner, uttering a high-pitched yipping noise and sometimes pausing to howl with the intensity of a minuscule wolf. When game is plentiful the rodent will eat half its weight a day for weeks on end and then subsist through leaner times on fat stored in its body and tail.

I never got close enough to a grasshopper mouse to offer it a tidbit, but I often fed chipmunks, perky little rascals about four inches long with a tail of roughly equal length. The so-called Badlands chipmunk (known a little farther west as the Black Hills chipmunk) is a slightly paler version of the least chipmunk, common in the plains and plateaus of Wyoming, northeast Utah and northwest Colorado, and is the only Badlands animal that will almost always eat from the human hand. It will also, if startled, bite the hand that feeds it: sharp rodent incisors, as many a tourist has discovered, can bare a finger to the bone.

I suppose if you stood still long enough you might get a magpie to snatch a morsel from your hand; but my personal conviction is that, given a choice, the magpie would rather steal than beg. This handsome bird even looks like a well-dressed robber baron, with its glossy-black and pure-white plumage and a slender, trailing tail as long as the bird's 10-inch body. Once, while traipsing around the Conata area southeast of Sage Creek basin, I finished the two ham sandwiches I had brought along and was about to take on a caramel-and-nut bar when I glimpsed a movement in the grass about 10 feet away, put down my candy bar and went to investigate. There was nothing at the spot where I had seen the grass wave. When I came back the candy bar was gone—and on a nearby tree, looking at me with immense impudence, was a magpie with the bar in its beak. I have no doubt that it later ate the whole thing, wrapper and all.

Compared to the rapacious magpie, the prairie dog is the acme of respectability. I spent a lot of time at a 44-acre prairie-dog town near Sage Creek and marveled at the complex life of this community based

A rodent-killing rogues' gallery eyes its domain for prey and possible enemies. The most eclectic of all prairie predators, the coyote will eat virtually anything living—or recently dead. The well-camouflaged bull snake fattens on mice, pocket gophers and ground squirrels. The badger, using its powerful claws, usually burrows after moles, marmots and other below-ground dwellers. And the nearly extinct black-footed ferret makes a living slithering down into prairie-dog holes to trap its victims off guard.

A COILED BULL SNAKE

A WARY BADGER

A COYOTE ON ALERT

A LITHE BLACK-FOOTED FERRET

on a high order of communication and interaction *(pages 108-123)*. The prairie dog is perhaps the only really abundant mammal in the Badlands, a remarkable achievement considering the number and variety of its enemies. There is a charming and persistent legend that snakes, burrowing owls and prairie dogs inhabit the same burrows in happy harmony. It isn't so. The snakes sometimes take over abandoned prairie-dog burrows, and the owls—stilt-legged birds, 9 to 10 inches long —often dig their own holes, though they prefer not to.

A marauding resident of the dog towns is the black-footed ferret, a lithe little creature with the grace of a tiny tiger, built like a weasel but with black feet and a masklike black band across its face. Naturalists have never had much chance to study the ferret, a shy nocturnal loner. Apparently it subsists almost entirely on prairie dogs, and when Great Plains cattle ranchers began, from the turn of the century to about 1925, systematically wiping out dog towns by wholesale poisoning, the ferret became exceedingly scarce. It is estimated that about 100 ferrets remain in South Dakota, but none have been sighted in Badlands National Monument for more than 15 years. The ranchers claimed that cattle broke their legs in prairie-dog holes and that the little animals ate scarce herbage. Actually, the prairie dogs probably did more good than harm. Their burrows aerated the land and in addition to grass the prairie dogs ate other plants that cattle disdained. But ranching is a hard business, full of adversities, like droughts and blizzards, that the rancher is powerless to control. Killing varmints helps ease frustrations. Wherever they have been let alone, as at Sage Creek, the prairie dogs have re-established themselves; but the ferret has not made a similar recovery and seems doomed.

Otherwise, except for the wolf and the bear, most of the animals that roamed the Badlands before the white man came are still there. The bobcat is prevalent; once in a while someone still sights a mountain lion. Elk are scarce, but there are plenty of mule deer. The Audubon bighorn sheep, a prime favorite among early pothunters, has been extinct since the 1920s, but an attempt has been made to replace it with a near relative, the Rocky Mountain bighorn sheep, about a dozen of which now survive in Badlands National Monument.

The monument also offers one of the remaining herds of the *Bison bison bison* whose repetitive scientific name serves to distinguish it from the *Bison bison athabascae,* the wood buffalo that still roams some Canadian forests. It has been estimated that at the time Columbus discovered what he thought were the Indies, some 60 million buffalo roamed North America and were even to be seen in Atlantic Coast forests and meadows. Within about 300 years after Columbus, burgeoning Eastern settlement had almost completely driven the lumbering beasts west of the Mississippi. Then the pace of destruction began accelerating; by the 1830s George Catlin, the pioneer Western painter, while marveling at the number of bison he saw on the Great Plains, was appalled by the "death and destruction that is dealt among these noble animals, and hurrying on their final extinction."

Catlin was almost right about the fate of the bison, which eventually was nearly wiped out by meat hunters, skin hunters, ranchers seeking range land, railroaders and soldiers trying to subdue the Indians by cutting off their main source of food. By the beginning of this century, despite growing protests and salvage efforts, only two wild herds were known to exist, one in Canada and one in Yellowstone National Park that numbered a mere 21 beasts. Fortunately, nearly 1,000 animals were kept alive by individual owners and by zoos. And from these frail resources, various protected Western herds—including 1,600 to 2,000 in the parks of North and South Dakota—now exist as reminders of the multitudes that Catlin saw.

Some 200 of these modern survivors are thriving behind fences in the Badlands. Not that fences mean an awful lot to a bison. An adult male may stand six feet at the hump and weighs close to a ton. When a Badlands bison decides to go somewhere, it goes—on occasion even to the outskirts of the town of Wall. For all his size, the bull bison can run 35 miles an hour and turn on a dime. He is absolutely unpredictable and has been known to attack out of sheer bad temper.

A direct confrontation with one of these monsters is, I can tell you, a paralyzing experience. Late one June afternoon I was walking down the bed of Sage Creek when I sensed a presence, though there was not a sound other than the eternal whispering of the Badlands wind. I stood stock still and slowly looked around. At first, nothing. And then, there they were: the bloodshot eyes of a bison bull, glaring at me through a bankside thicket of—appropriately—buffaloberry bushes (bison occasionally scratch themselves on the plant's thorny branches). My knowledge that the beast would have to crash down over a steep eight-foot-high bank to get at me was small comfort. Still less comforting was a sudden memory: I recalled that the famed naturalist Ernest Thompson Seton had rated the bison even ahead of the grizzly as North America's most dangerous mammal. The bison and I stood there, eyeball to eyeball, as it were, for what seemed like a lifetime. Finally the giant gave a terrifying snort, cleared out its nostrils with a single swipe of its long purplish tongue and rumbled away through the thicket.

While the bison had to be artificially reintroduced to the Badlands, the pronghorn—driven out at about the same time and for much the same reasons—has returned on its own and seems to be flourishing. Its resurgence is a special delight, for the handsome tan-and-white animal, sleekly built and possessed of dazzling speed, is a pride of the prairies. Weighing about 100 pounds, the pronghorn looks and runs like an antelope and is commonly so called, but is actually a separate species —*Antilocapra americana,* literally, the American goat antelope.

I got my first sight of a pronghorn one morning in May with ranger Jim Wilson, who was on patrol in the monument. We were driving along a gravel road when we spotted a pronghorn doe browsing in a nearby thicket. Jim pointed out her flaccid underbelly, a sure sign, he said, that she had given birth not long before. We knew that in all probability twin kids were hidden a couple of hundred feet apart in the deep grass. Does usually bear twins and separate the newborn in this way, so that if a predator gets one it may miss the other.

Pronghorn kids need not hide for long, however. After four days they can outrun any man; within a week they are keeping pace with their mother. This is no easy task, since the pronghorn is the speediest of all North American animals, bounding along in 12- to 20-foot leaps at 45 miles per hour and able to accelerate rapidly but briefly up to 60 miles per hour when really alarmed. The pronghorn's heavily muscled legs are built for speed; its lungs and windpipe are oversized for deep, fast breathing; and its heart, designed to pump blood rapidly under the strain of running, is twice as big as that of other animals of similar weight. Often, when traveling by Jeep across roadless tracts of prairie, I encountered small bands of pronghorns that seemed to make a sport of their speed, playfully quartering back and forth in front of me and easily staying ahead although I was driving about 20 miles per hour.

The pronghorn's speed is only one of its superb qualifications for survival. It does not seriously compete for food with the other two great consumers of prairie plant life, the prairie dog and the bison. Rather, the pronghorn relishes the weedy forbs, such as sweet clover and cudweed sagewort, that take over when other animals have eaten grasses down to the root. With evident enjoyment and without apparent adverse effect, the pronghorn even eats the prickly pear, spines and all.

Masked like the executioners they are, these burrowing owls make their deadly forays against rodents, insects and prairie-dog pups.

Its eyesight is a natural marvel, estimated as equivalent to that of a man with five-power binoculars. Such eyes enable the animal to spot an enemy's approach from several miles across the prairie. When danger seems near, the pronghorn warns its fellows through a signaling system like that of the white-tailed deer: its long, white rump hairs bristle, fanning out like a gigantic powder puff, flashing a signal that other pronghorns can see for miles.

The pronghorn's fatal flaw is curiosity. It seems compelled to investigate almost anything that attracts its attention—a handkerchief on the end of a stick, even the boots of a hunter lying on his back and waving his feet in the air. It is hardly surprising that the more than 40 million pronghorns that browsed the prairies in the early 1800s had been reduced by 1924 to only about 27,000, virtually none of them in the Badlands. Today, attracted by the protection offered in South Dakota's Badlands National Monument and North Dakota's Theodore Roosevelt National Memorial Park, the pronghorn has returned and its combined population in the two states has leveled off at about 12,000.

Of all the Badlands animals whose daily lives I observed, I think a family of ferruginous hawks brought me my most rewarding encounter. Their nest, a rather haphazard construction of twigs, sticks and branches, was in a cleft high on the White River cliffside near the swallows' colony. In the nest by late June were four nestlings, all the size of fat chicken hens and all ravenous. They kept the father ranging far and wide in quest of food for his famished family. I saw him several times —easily identifiable by a notch in his tail where several feathers were missing—soaring over the prairie-dog town at Sage Creek, at least 25 miles from his nest. Despite his ferocious appearance, he never did very well in his Sage Creek shopping, as far as I could see.

For all his ill luck at the dog town, my hawk rarely arrived home empty taloned. He returned several times a day to the nest, usually with a small rodent—not nearly enough food to appease the appetites of the hungry chicks. They could be heard squawking their displeasure for a considerable distance. Only twice did I see the male return with the prideful air that betokened a hearty meal. Once he bore a large jack rabbit. On another occasion it was a three-foot-long plains garter snake with gleaming black skin and a bright-orange stripe running the length of its back. The hawk may have paid a price for that catch; when attacked, the plains garter snake has the uncouth habit of smearing its antagonist with a malodorous secretion from an anal gland. The baby hawks, however, apparently never noticed the smell.

While the male hawk was foraging, his mate kept vigil, sometimes from the nest itself, occasionally from a cottonwood lookout post across the river and most often in long, slow circular sweeps through the sky above. Any human approach to within a quarter of a mile was met by a scream of rage and anxiety as the bird flew in lower, smaller circles centering on the stranger. Although the female flapped about in a most threatening manner, she never approached closer than about 50 feet.

Some weeks later the little hawks were almost ready to fly. For days they perched on the edge of the nest, flapping their wings in imitation of flight. But despite the vocal urgings of their parents, they seemed unwilling to launch themselves on the great venture that would forever change their lives. On a raw, rainy morning, with dark clouds scudding low across the sky and a cold wind gusting up to 50 miles an hour, photographer Enrico Ferorelli and I decided to approach the nest from the top of the cliff. This required driving a short distance on a country road, then walking across nearly a mile of hilly grassland and belly crawling out to peer down over the edge of a crumbly cliff overhang. Meanwhile, the wind blew and the rain fell and the angry mother hawk flew around making menacing noises.

Our activity unfortunately frightened the nestlings, and one of them lurched from the nest in premature first flight, half gliding and half falling, to land with a large plop on a mudbank across the river. There it stayed, either stuck or simply unable to take off in the face of the high wind. Determined to save the hawk, we returned to the campground, picked up a large cardboard box and slogged to the spot in the deep mud where it was stranded. When we finally arrived, the bird was gone. All that remained was a depression in the mud and a greenish blob of dung. To this day I have not the slightest idea what we could have done had we found the little hawk still there. I suppose that we had the notion of taking it up to the top of the bluff and then attempting to drop it back down into the nest, a tricky maneuver that might or might not have worked. But now, as we looked skyward, there were three soaring hawks—father, mother and the former nestling, having the time of its life.

It was a great thing to see.

The Sociable Prairie Dog

PHOTOGRAPHS BY JIM BRANDENBURG

No Badlands wild creature seems to manage life better than that sociable citizen, the prairie dog. It constructs large towns, while avoiding overcrowding and pollution. When not looking after its family and home, it sensibly spends its time in eating and snoozing, or kissing, cuddling up to and caressing its kin.

For millennia this amiable rodent burrowed through millions of Great Plains acres, surviving bitter winters, sizzling summers, prairie fires, cloudbursts—and plagues of predators including hawks, snakes, ferrets, eagles, badgers, coyotes and hungry Indians.

Subsequently wiped out in many places by ranchers whose cattle competed with it for grass, the animal now flourishes only in protected areas such as Wind Cave National Park, home of the posturing, yodeling householder at right. Here at the edge of South Dakota's Badlands thousands of *Cynomys ludovicianus,* or black-tailed prairie dogs, have spread their intricate burrows over some 75 acres of grassland.

Prairie-dog family activity centers around the so-called coterie—a unit consisting of one or more males, several consorts and litters of up to 10 pups. Each coterie controls an area of about three quarters of an acre within a dog town. Underground burrows, averaging about 24 feet of tunnel for each entrance, widen into a series of chambers used as nests, storage rooms and toilets. The temperature inside a burrow remains fairly constant the year round, and is always warmer than the outside air in winter and cooler in summer. During Badlands summers this air conditioning is vital for prairie dogs, which perish quickly if exposed for any length of time to the heat of a 100° F. day. Most burrows have at least two entrances, so that if a snake or a ferret slips in by one door, the tenants can slip out by the other.

A mound of dirt up to a foot high surrounding each entrance keeps out surface water, and provides an elevation from which a prairie dog can scan its domain and bark out warnings of approaching predators or, more often, defiantly shrill an assertion of its territorial rights.

Lavishly affectionate with friends, it distrusts all prairie dogs outside its own coterie. Alert to repel threatening intruders, the prairie dog not only guards its own burrows but may travel up to three miles a day waddling around the jealously maintained border of the coterie.

Stretched to its full 17-inch height, with nose aloft and its back arched, a prairie dog sounds the two-note territorial call warning all strangers off its turf. The same call is used as an all-clear signal and is answered by others in the coterie. To spring onto tiptoes takes practice—youngsters often take pratfalls while trying it.

Two members of a prairie-dog coterie exchange a greeting kiss atop a mound. In each group, the first one home welcomes all the others.

Snarls for Strangers, Kisses for Kin

Periodically, two prairie dogs within a coterie will stop eating or digging and rush to press their mouths together. This practice is standard in a dog town, where all clan members kiss frequently. The gesture may consist of just a passing peck; or it can be an osculatory marathon in which first one prairie dog and then the other rolls on its back in seeming ecstasy until both finally go off to feed, shoulder to shoulder.

Any prairie dog rejecting a kiss is instantly suspect as an interloper. Snarling, the animal that offered the kiss lifts and spreads its tail in righteous wrath—and immediately gets either a return kiss or a confrontation. If the suspect proves not to be just an absent-minded fellow clansman but an invader trying to extend its coterie's lebensraum, a ritual clash ensues. Tails up, the two prairie dogs crouch and circle. First one and then the other presents its rear for a ceremonial smelling of its anal glands. Such encounters usually end in quick mutual disengagement. But even if the crisis escalates and one prairie dog nips the other's rump, the battle rarely results in moving a boundary more than a few inches.

Two strangers meeting by chance near an invisible but closely defended territorial border between coteries (top), stage the formal confrontation that such encounters demand. With tail raised, one animal turns its back (center) and presents its hindquarters for an exploratory sniff (bottom).

With one foot in its burrow to ensure
a rapid retreat, a prairie dog sounds
a warning bark as it sights a hereditary
enemy, the coyote. The alarm will
usually be repeated, and heeded by all
prairie dogs within earshot until the
threat to the community has vanished.

On this occasion, the enemy turns out
to be a 10-week-old coyote pup. Driven
more likely by curiosity than by
hunger, the pup is a minor menace
—but even so, it spells danger to
the diminutive prairie dog; and it looms
larger with every hesitant stride.

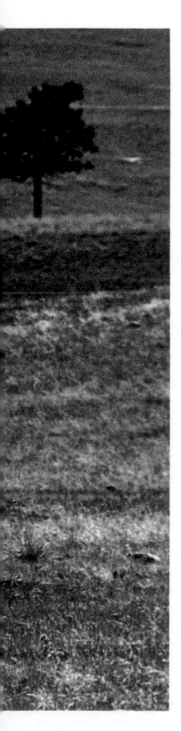

An Unremitting Communal Vigilance

Though prairie dogs may gang up on an invading ferret and try to bury it alive by sealing it in a burrow, their best defense is in the coterie's unremitting communal vigilance. When the prairie dogs shear down tall weeds around their towns for food, they also reduce the cover for approaching predators. They constantly watch earth and sky through bulging eyes whose orange lenses filter intense sunlight, and which are set high on the head—almost as good as a periscope for letting a prairie dog peek unseen from a burrow.

A prairie dog that sights anything it considers to be suspicious sounds a warning. In fact, prairie dogs are compulsive vocalizers, even in their sleep. And they might well live in constant panic had they not learned to ignore alarmists who bark at butterflies, and to recognize at least 10 different calls. One kind of yelp, rapidly relayed through the town, simply alerts everybody. At a different cry that means imminent danger —like a swooping hawk—all prairie dogs dive for the nearest burrow. Only in these emergencies do the householders admit strange adults.

As the coyote draws nearer, the prairie dog drops lower and lower into its burrow, still barking the alarm and keeping its eyes riveted on the approaching enemy. A veteran of numerous violent encounters, as shown by the scars on its face, the prairie dog waits till the last second and then abruptly vanishes, leaving a puzzled pup peering in at the empty entrance.

A prairie dog, deftly using its front paws like a pair of hands, tears pieces from a prickly thistle leaf and lifts them to its mouth.

Converting Fodder to Winter Fat

Prairie dogs are voracious, efficient herbivores, although they also consume insects and worm larvae. However, they are particularly fond of broad-leafed weeds, as well as seeds and grasses. Their sharp incisors easily shear stems and roots, which their broad molars grind into digestible wads. As another helper in the quick production of nourishment, the prairie dog has a large reservoir called the caecum inside its pear-shaped abdomen. It works with the stomach to convert fodder into fat.

Since a prairie dog rarely grazes more than 300 feet away from its burrow, the natural increase in a colony's population would quickly exhaust the lushest prairie larder. The animals avert this Malthusian fate by migrating in small numbers, as the population grows, to create new coteries on the town's outskirts.

The prairie dog needs every bite it can get. Water is scarce in most dog towns, so the animals rely on juices of plants like thistles for liquids. And they must accumulate as much fat as they can carry to help last through the winter.

Some mountain species hibernate from fall to spring; the South Dakota blacktails merely work shorter hours in winter, conserving energy in long rest periods. They pop out of their burrows to sunbathe whenever weather permits, sample the dry, winter-killed herbage, and with the strong claws of their forefeet, dig swiftly into the cold earth for roots.

Replete but alert after a meal at a weed patch, the prairie dog slumps to rest on its rump.

Prairie dogs, like this one combing its mother's fur, seem born with the grooming knack.

Stretched out in an attitude of deep content, a pup relaxes to a sibling's soothing touch.

The Social Rite of Grooming

From infancy onward, a prairie dog's tawny coat is subject to constant, intensive grooming by others of its kind. This act of using the long, curved front teeth for gently combing out another prairie dog's fur is a habit as deeply ingrained in the animal's nature as eating or kissing. Pups seem to acquire it instinctively. They toddle about insisting on grooming every prairie dog in sight —siblings, friends, parents, relatives, neighbors and even strangers.

Grooming obviously removes dirt and such parasites as fleas, and also seems to provide the prairie dogs with a satisfaction greater than the joys of cleanliness. Prairie-dog pups raised in captivity, free of dirt and insects, still groom sedulously.

Most importantly, grooming appears to be a vital part of the prairie dog's complex social structure. Being highly dependent on its fellows, a prairie dog apparently needs frequent reassurance that it is among friends. But as with kissing, it also seems to find grooming fun. A kiss may lead to pawing, nibbling or to grooming. If the groomer pauses, its partner nudges it into action.

The urge to eat seems to take a prairie dog's mind off grooming entirely. As summer slides into autumn, the grooming passion lapses, almost as though every prairie dog were now intent on using every minute for cramming down the last of the fast-fading greenery in anticipation of the lean days ahead.

In this family tableau, a mother patiently grooms one of her litter, while submitting to the nuzzlings of two other offspring.

Fly-bitten bison seeking dust baths wallow their way through a dog town, destroying burrows before the eyes of the dismayed residents.

Patient Repairs for a Bulldozed Burrow

As trying as any hazard in a prairie dog's life must be a summer visit from a bumbling herd of bison. Unconcerned with the physical or social structure of the dog town, the bison are looking for a good dust wallow. They have shed their winter wool, and insects are attacking their relatively unprotected hides.

The dog-town mounds—sheared of vegetation and neatly heaped up —are eminently inviting. The bison scatter the mounds with horns and hoofs. They level it, roll in it—and acquire a protective coat of dust.

The bison may hang around, disrupting the town's life, for an hour or a week before moving on. The prairie dogs wait it out, and after the next rain makes the soil cohesive and workable, they patiently reconstruct their mounds, pushing with their paws to heap up the towers of dirt. Only if the bison return repeatedly will the prairie dogs give up and move a burrow entrance.

Even an outrage like a bison onslaught, however, has its favorable aspects. Bison may leave a dog town looking bulldozed, but the churned-up earth will soon produce new and more bountiful crops of the grasses and broad-leafed herbs that are the prairie dogs' favorite foods.

In repairing its burrow, a prairie dog paws the earth back into a mound (above right), and then tamps with its nose. From time to time, dried grasses are gathered (bottom) for use in relining the nest of the burrow.

The Wonderful World of the Prairie Pup

In early June young prairie dogs emerge from their natal burrows into a wonderful world. Abrim with energy, they wrestle with siblings and friends, try to kiss and groom every prairie dog they meet—and find all adults delightfully indulgent.

Females will obligingly suckle any pup that comes by; and when a pup fumblingly attempts, as many do, to suckle a male, the older prairie dog gently turns the youngster over and soothingly grooms its belly fur. Only the most importunate pup will ever draw a nip, a kick or pummeling from an elder, some of whom will even emigrate to escape the juveniles rather than punish them. Pups are welcome in any burrow, including one in a strange coterie from which their parents would be ejected; and it is some time before a pup learns that only certain burrows are home. Under such communal care, few pups die in their first year.

Throughout the summer the pup learns the boundaries of its coterie, the code of signals, and which plants to eat. By fall it is nearly as big as its parents. By next summer it will be ready to launch a new coterie.

Three playful pups work off energy in a tussle that ends in a tangle of heads and limbs. During the frolic one of the siblings backs off to watch for a moment, turns away for a bit of digging, and then, as its mates unscramble, rushes up to assert kinship with a kiss (far right). In games, the pups gain strength and coordination while practicing their social skills.

Two youngsters romp at the end of a long day's kissing, grooming, eating and playing, while their parents relax in the light of the setting

sun. *The prairie dogs are diurnal creatures, easily disoriented at night; soon all will retire to the safety and the quiet of their burrows.*

5/ The Bountiful Grasses

*Grass is the forgiveness
of nature — her constant benediction.*

SENATOR JOHN JAMES INGALLS/ 1872

Grass is life in the Badlands. To the creatures that move amid the wind-bent stems, that fly above, that burrow beneath its roots, grass is food or shelter or both. Grass is also the bond that helps to hold together the surface of the earth. And in this austere region, while giving generously of its bounty, the grass wages an unending but successful struggle for its own life. I walked along dry gullies in the Badlands and saw tufts of grass, cheerfully plumed with seeds, springing up from hard-edged cracks in seemingly lifeless clay. Where the waters of the creeks had cut into the banks, I could see that the black crust of soil at the top was less than one quarter of an inch thick; grass thrived there.

The most striking monuments to the toughness of grass are the sod tables that rise above the crumbled rock of the Badlands—each table representing a bit of prairie saved from the erosive waters for a few hundred or a few thousand years by its crown of green grass. Sheep Mountain Table *(pages 60-61)*, where late-arriving homesteaders, desperate for the last bits of cheap land, once tried to scrape a living out of the sod, is but one dramatic example of a place where the hardy, resilient grasses have kept the soil together. Elsewhere, such as in the White River Valley at the dying town of Imlay, the grasses have reclaimed and restored the battered earth. An empty corral, its posts broken and its barbed wire sagging, stands here next to a tiny shack alongside the railroad tracks. For decades the hoofs of thousands of cattle tore up the sod at this livestock loading station and turned the ground into a wallow of mud and clay. No trainloads of cattle have been shipped from Imlay for 40 years; no passenger train has stopped at Imlay in more than 20 years. Grass now covers all.

But the grass here is not—and never was—the towering, majestic growth that once flourished on the prairie to the east, stretching from the wooded borders of Indiana into Iowa; there the "flaunting grass," as Washington Irving called it, grew eight feet tall. Though some relatively tall strains do grow in the Badlands—leafy big bluestem, golden Indian grass, tenacious needle-and-thread—their stems rarely achieve a height of more than two or three feet. Nor is this region part of the higher, drier short-grass steppe that adjoins it to the west, where most of the grasses curl close to the ground, fading into sagebrush to the south, and, in the north, gradually giving way to the aspen and spruce forests of Canada. Rather, the Badlands is mixed-grass country, a land where the stresses of climate constantly try the resourcefulness of the grass, forcing the strains to adapt to the demands of the environment.

At first glance this grassland can appear forbidding in its unsheltered vastness. And indeed for some 70 years after the Louisiana Purchase, the section of the plains west of the Missouri River was called the Great American Desert. Early pioneers shied away from the frighteningly exposed landscape with its sparse trees tucked along creek beds, sucking up precious moisture whenever a cloudburst filled the gullies. But the grassland only appeared as desert in the eyes of farmers and other settlers accustomed to the rolling green hills of the East. Others saw a thrilling expanse of free and bountiful land. As long ago as 1804 Meriwether Lewis, of the Lewis and Clark expedition, climbed a high ridge on the Missouri River just north of its conjunction with the White River, looked west and reported in his unique grammar: "The shortness and virdue of grass gave the plain the appearance throughout it's whole extent of beatifull bowling-green in fine order . . . this senery already rich and pleasing and beatiful was still farther hightened by immence herds of Buffaloe, deer Elk and Antelopes which we saw in every direction feeding on the hills and plains. I do not think I exagerate when I estimate the number of Buffaloe which could be compreed at one view to amount to 3,000."

Most of the creatures are gone now. But the grassland itself is still, to me at least, much as Meriwether Lewis first saw it—pleasing and beautiful and endlessly fascinating. Over 40 species of grass now grow in the Badlands, and it is this rich variety that gives the grassland its

A western meadowlark, perched near a shell-leafed penstemon that sprouts above the prairie grasses, trills its rich, flutelike melody.

strength, that enables it to rejuvenate itself and, ultimately, to survive. I tramped through a small sector of this grassland early one June morning, when the ground cover reflected a kaleidoscope of subtle hues: pale yellow, silvery lavender, orangey brown were streaked through the green. And the green appeared in a hundred shades. The taller grasses bent and swayed before the westerly wind; the shorter grasses moved in a harmonious rhythm. Willa Cather once described the effect: "I felt that the grass was the country, as the water is the sea. . . . And there was so much motion in it; the whole country seemed, somehow, to be running."

I set out early from my camp on the south bank of the White River and headed toward the first sharp ridges of the Great Wall, four miles to the north. My route traversed an almost continuous stretch of grass, broken only in a few places by rock outcrops and low sod tables and by the inevitable barbed-wire fence that marked each mile section. Cottonwoods lined my starting place along the riverbank, intermingled with thickets of meadow rose, wild plum and buffaloberry; these were the last trees or bushes I would pass all morning.

The grass began immediately, and I noticed the taller varieties first: tufts of sand dropseed, nodding Canada wild rye and little bluestem. This bluestem was the most abundant grass on the plains before the settlers came, but now it exists only in random patches. Its dark green stalks rise about two feet from the ground. Here by the White River the bluestem emerged from a thick tuft of leaves; the roots were probably thrust five feet or more into the fine-textured soil. I tore off one of the blades, and as I held it in my hand against the low, early morning light I could see that the underside was covered with white hairlike tendrils. This wispy growth is a defense mechanism the bluestem has in common with many other prairie grasses; the hairs baffle the dry wind as it passes through the grass, slowing the rate of evaporation and conserving the plant's store of moisture.

Little bluestem has another way of resisting desiccation. During dry spells its leaves roll in on themselves, reducing the exposed blade surface and further lowering the rate of evaporation. In that state of botanical hibernation, a stand of little bluestem takes on a hoary, wizened look, but the grass can endure for dry summer after dry summer. When the rains finally return, the blades unfold; the bluestem and the prairie turn green again.

Soon I found myself walking through a stand of stiffly erect grass that was curiously uniform both in its greenish-blue color and its height of about three feet. This was western wheat grass, a sturdy prairie native that can completely dominate a field when conditions are right —which they were on this semiarid acre of flat river plain.

I was midway through the wheat grass when I was brought up short by a painful, prickly sensation in the lower part of my leg just above my low boot tops. I thought at first the pinpricks were insect bites, but when I bent down to investigate I found dozens of thin, yellow tendrils dangling from my socks. As I looked closer I saw that the end of each four-inch tendril was a barbed seed with a sharp point poking right into my skin. Without noticing, I had walked through a scattering of needle-and-thread grass and had become ensnared in its complex method of propagation.

This grass, also appropriately known as porcupine grass, is one of the most tenacious and vigorous inhabitants of the prairie; fossil seeds similar to the modern variety have been found with those of the small three-toed horse that roamed the area of the Badlands some 20 million years ago. Each year when the seeds strip away from the mature grass stem—usually in early summer—they come off with their tough, three-or-four-inch filament tightly twisted like newly spun thread. The filament catches the wind, helping to loft the seeds away. Then, when the point of the seed finds a target—soil, preferably, but any intermediate host such as my sock or a buffalo's hide will do—the barb takes hold and keeps the seed fastened in place.

Once the seed has lodged itself, the filament begins its second chore. As the surrounding atmosphere moistens with rain or dew, the twisted filament expands and uncoils; when the air dries, the tendril coils again. Each twisting movement drills the seed farther and farther into its new home until the seed is well planted and can germinate. After every subsequent walk through the prairie, while the needle-and-thread grass was in seed, I pulled 20 or more seeds out of my socks; Lord knows how many more I jostled off the stems and dropped along the way. This is an intriguingly effective system of reproduction. Yet I find it perhaps no more remarkable than the ingenious fecundity of *every* kind of prairie grass.

Grasses are a new kind of life on the earth if measured on the broadest scale of evolution. The first tufts probably appeared in North America only 40 million years ago, long after the Black Hills had started to rise, and the ancient sea bed from which they emerged had been replaced by a semitropical forest and a flowering plain. This lush vegetation, flourishing in a very mild and uniform climate, eventually was replaced by the earliest grasses, which probably resembled bamboo. The genial climate of this region gradually gave way to sharply defined seasons, with harsher, drier conditions. The new plants adapted, multiplied and flourished.

During various times of recurring drought, temperature change and floods, the response of the grasses was to shed their frills, strip down to basic structure, and toughen up. They abandoned the showy, scented flowers of their ancestors, and in the process they also abandoned the flowers' dependence on insects for transportation. Grasses now depend for the most part on a more powerful and direct means of spreading their seed: the wind. Furthermore, they have become mostly self-pollinating. In the grasses, each flower has been reduced to a tiny, essential fragment—a single fruit fused to a single seed and covered by a thin, scaly hull. Once planted, the hull disintegrates, exposing the embryo plant—a core of concentrated protein, carbohydrates and oil. The hull is chaff; the core is new life.

Yet even this elegant simplification of design was not enough to ensure the triumphant survival of the grasses on an increasingly rigorous planet. And many of them developed a backup system to perpetuate life even if, for one reason or another, the seed crop should fail for a year or so. In other plants, such as the broad-leafed flowering varieties, the growing tissue is at the tip of the stem; if the stem is cut or destroyed, the plant can become sterile. But in grasses, the growth is from below, as it is in human hair. In addition, many species of grass can colonize adjacent bare soil by developing buds at the base of the plant. These buds extend into so-called runners, which grow horizontally, either above or below the ground, sending up sprouts of new grass as they move. Thus, when the tip of a grass stem is cut—by a grazing animal, by fire, or by a scythe—the grass continues to grow.

This sidewise creep of the prairie grasses, combined with a dense network of roots, eventually builds the tough, living structure called sod. The resilient mat of sod I felt underfoot on my walk was about four inches thick, created mostly by low-lying grasses I had so far overlooked—buffalo grass and blue grama. Both strains curled close to the ground, only three to five inches high, intermingled here and there with tall bluestem and wheat grass. The tight turf made by these short grasses husbands each drop of rain and shelters it from the drying wind. The roots have an exceptionally high concentration of tiny membranes

The floor of Burns Basin lies flat and green between the steeply eroded flanks of its embracing walls. Watered by tributaries of the White River and by infrequent rains, the basin floor is covered predominantly by little-bluestem and blue-grama grasses.

through which water and minerals pass from the pores of the reluctant clay soil into the plant. During prolonged droughts, many other plants may die before they can extract and absorb the last remaining molecules of life-saving moisture still locked in the earth. The well-adapted buffalo grass and grama, however, can survive two or three years of severe drought and then, when the rain finally does fall, they come back as vigorous as ever.

Early Texas cattle ranchers discovered these magic qualities of grama and buffalo grass. As the cattlemen expanded their herds, they followed the grass northward, helping to colonize the high plains and in the process putting an end to the legend of the Great American Desert. Land and cattle investors as far away as London and Edinburgh began receiving regular reports on the thriving condition of the pasture along the Cheyenne River. By the last quarter of the 19th Century, hundreds of thousands of young steers were driven up from Texas each summer to spend two or three years fattening on the nutritious Dakota grasses before making the final train trip to the Chicago stockyards.

After the cattlemen came the homesteaders, who were given powerful impetus by a Congressional act of 1889 that turned over nine million acres of Indian territory to white settlement. This became one of the last major stretches of land left on the American frontier, and the homesteaders who headed for the Badlands were among the last of the pioneers. Farmers who had failed in the East, sons of poor farm families whose meager acreage could support no more adults, and men and women fleeing the harsh life of factory cities came west to the Badlands for a final chance on the land.

They plowed the soil for their crops. And finding no timber on the open spaces they learned to raise the ground itself over their heads for shelter. Teams of oxen dragging special sod plows cut long strips into the virgin sod. Then the mat of grass and soil was chopped into rectangles about a foot wide and two feet long. From these crude bricks of turf the people built sod houses called soddies, the first homes of many a pioneer family on the Badlands prairies.

In the decade from 1900 to 1910, the prairie around the Badlands became dotted with soddies and tar-paper shacks; and the population of western South Dakota tripled. Farmers ripped up more soil to plant cash crops. And though their efforts were mighty, the fruits were small. Ten acres of oats yielded one homesteader only six dollars in 1912, as compared to an average of $88 earned elsewhere in the United States. Such crops turned out to be far more vulnerable than were the hardy

The spherical growths on these plants are galls, formed when insect larvae hatch within the plants' tissues. The galls at top, resembling prickly fruits, have supplanted some of the leaves on a wild rose. Below, a gall balloons from a dead goldenrod stem.

buffalo grass and grama to the rigors of Badlands climate. Moreover, the plowed soil was exposed to the powerful winds of the plain. Within a single generation the delicate balance that had sustained the prairie for millions of years was tipped.

Some botanists have called this balance climax grassland, suggesting that a rough but perfectly adapted mixture of just the right grasses has come to rest on just the right soil in just the right climate. And indeed it had, having acquired over the millennia an ability to survive in a soil that was swept by wind, dried by drought, burned by the sun, drowned by sudden rains, turned to ash by prairie fires, trampled by millions of bison and pronghorns, and torn up by the burrows of hundreds of millions of prairie dogs and badgers. The climax grasses not only survived; they adjusted and thrived amid this threatened destruction.

As droughts came and went, the short grasses, grama and buffalo grass, took over; and where the short grass had grown, sagebrush and mesquite crowned the land. Then, with a cycle of heavy rains, the tall grasses moved into their territory, while the short grasses held on in patches or retreated farther to the west. The grazing animals and the fires, meanwhile, swept away the accumulation of seasonal litter that would otherwise have suffocated the parent grasses. Instead, room was made for new seeds to drill into the rich humus and for new runners to grow along the ground. And if the bison grazed a section of the grassland too closely and the grass there started to die, the animals moved across the open country; the injured grass had years to recover—and it did. Thus, the climactic balance of prairie-grass life was not static but resulted, instead, from a continuous reaction to life-threatening change. And the balance could be accomplished only over a long enough time and in a space that was big enough.

Then this balance was overturned by the plow and the impatience of man. The farmers' dreams of plenty amid the grass fields of the Badlands blew away with the drought and dust storms of the 1930s. By that time, the wounded and overworked grass cover was no longer bonded to the earth by a network of roots and runners. When the rains failed in 1933 and again in 1934, the dry soil simply lifted off; in some places the wind tore away soil so far below the surface that rocks which the farmers' plows had never reached were exposed. In May of 1934, when the wind howled out of the west, the fine-textured soil of the Badlands joined that of Kansas, Texas and Oklahoma and blew so far east that it darkened the sun over New York City at midday, drifted

A 25-to-30-year-old prickly-pear cactus, whose lengthy branches suggest its age, spreads out along a clay embankment.

onto the desk of President Roosevelt in the White House and dropped eventually on the decks of ships 300 miles offshore in the Atlantic.

The scars of that era have largely been erased by now. Much of the native prairie grass through which I walked that early summer morning has been carefully rescued or restored, and is now lovingly sheltered by the National Park Service and the U.S. Forest Service. The guardianship by the Park Service has been so zealous, in fact, that in places the hardy native grass is beginning to falter like an overprotected child. With no grazing herds of buffalo and no natural fires (they are put out by rangers as fast as they flare), a stifling layer of litter has been accumulating faster than the sparse moisture of the Badlands can reduce it by decay.

Under these conditions, each succeeding year's crop of grass is likely to be thinner and more vulnerable. When the native bluestem or grama finally gives way, the seeds of so-called invader grasses move in to take their place. These new seeds are borne in principally by wind currents that carry large quantities of them through the atmosphere as high as 8,000 feet above the continent. Stonyhill muhly grass, native to the Eastern states, and Japanese brome, a Eurasian grass strain first introduced to the United States on the East and West coasts, were both unknown to the Badlands 150 years ago. Now they both thrive there. Birds also carry the newcomer seeds on their long migrations, lodged in dried mud on their feet.

Some of the seeds are inadvertently brought here by man. A few years ago botanist Ted Van Bruggen, a leading authority on the flora of the northern plains, found on the South Dakota plain some blades of a foot-high, yellow-spiked grass that puzzled him because he could not immediately identify it. However, he was certain that this was a grass he'd never seen before in this area. "I quickly discovered," said Van Bruggen, "that it was *Polypogon,* or rabbit-foot grass, which usually grows in states south and southwest of the Badlands and had never been previously reported in South Dakota. I decided to try to find out how it got here. In checking with the Corps of Engineers which had just built two dams nearby on the Missouri River, I found that the heavy machinery they used had come from Arizona. The machines probably carried those seeds with them over all those miles."

Other invader plants also mingle today with the indigenous grasses. Usually, they gain a foothold only where the soil is broken—by wheels on a dirt road, by the cut of a plow, or by the relentless force of an eroding stream. And when they come, they stitch bright shades into the subtle coloring of the green carpet.

As I tramped through a sweep of grass, my eye was suddenly caught by a wide, parti-colored ribbon that unfurled before me. I walked closer and saw the ruts of an old homesteader's trail, now abandoned and overgrown with a gaudy array of grassland flowers. Clumps of reddish-stemmed Russian thistle bordered the road. For centuries, this pseudo-thistle plagued the peasants of the Russian steppes, choking out their crops with its prolific growth. Then, around 1880, some thistle seeds sprouted in South Dakota; inadvertently they had become mixed in with Russian flaxseed and planted by an innovative homesteader. By the turn of the century, this wiry variety of tumbleweed had established itself firmly in 16 western states and in Canada.

To the present generation of ranchers in the Badlands area, as to Europe's peasants of old, the Russian thistle is a pest with no redeeming virtue. To ranchers' parents, however, the invincible thistle revealed itself as one small gift from the dying prairie of the 1930s. When the native grasses were stripped away and the planted crops had wilted and died, the thistle grew. During those dark days, desperate ranchers cut down the thistles in the spring when the plants were young and tender and raked the stems into stacks of forage for their thirsty, starving livestock. It was meager fare, but it was something. Nowadays, ranchers concentrate their efforts on destroying the weed in those vulnerable first weeks of life before it matures and tumbles away, drifting seed into every open wound on the range. On this deserted old road, though, the thistle had eluded its enemies and was thriving.

A rowdy company of flowering weeds surrounded the thistles. Prominent in the crowd was the prickly-stemmed buffalo bur, an extremely aggressive, drought-resistant annual that I have seen thrive and flower even in a heavily used cattle corral. The buffalo bur's tiny yellow flowers marked the road clearly as it stretched into the prairie toward the east and west. And I recognized the splashes of pink along the road as creeping Jenny, which wound along the ground like a vine, and as the jaunty, foot-high clusters of bouncing Bet. Named after women in a less self-conscious age, perhaps because of their fragile beauty or maybe because of their fierce tenacity, both of these flowers cheerfully dapple what agronomists choose to call distressed prairie surfaces.

Most of the time, the flowers of the Badlands live out their lives as solitary individuals, somehow surviving in a world dominated by the lordly grasses. For me there is a rare kind of beauty in the fierce strength of these lonely flowers and in the frailty of their gently colored blooms. Each flower has to fight against overwhelming odds for its niche in place and time. I found a tufted evening-primrose, blossoming just an inch or so above a bare clay slope in the bleakest part of the Badlands. The bloom is short lived; within a day the large white petals would turn pink and wilt. And on another trek later in the summer, when most of the Badlands flowers had long since dried up, I saw a single, ten-petaled blazing star standing sentinel on an eroded creek bank, opening its pale yellow flower to the night-flying insects.

My journey across the prairie was almost over. I was nearing the tattered margin of the grasses, where the rocks of the Badlands surfaced. Prickly-pear cactus marked the border between grass and gravel; the notoriously tough cactus thrives under extreme conditions, growing where other vegetation fails to survive. Near the cactus a small soapweed stood bristling above the thinning grass. I shook the tall stalk with its creamy white flowers and a swarm of tiny white moths flew out, then quickly settled back again among the fleshy petals. They made me think that here, at the grim edge of life itself, life flourished.

The Great Wall brooded just ahead of me. I rested now against one of the mounds of rock that were strewn all around, and looked back at the four-mile stretch of grassland I had crossed. What started as a casual stroll had turned into my discovery of a universe of life—a glimpse into a wild abundance of colors, forms, struggles, victories and defeats. The midday sun now blazed over the grass, erasing all gentleness and all particulars. The shades and shapes of the prairie merged into a billowing mass and I experienced a sensation of unity, a momentary understanding of the complex patterns of growth and death and regeneration that add up to that single entity called the grassland.

A Rich Mosaic of Growing Things

PHOTOGRAPHS BY ENRICO FERORELLI

To most men who come upon the Western grasslands, the overwhelming impression is one of space, a limitless sweep of prairie that encircles the beholder, isolating and exposing him beneath the dome of the sky. Then there is the wind, pressing across the grass (right) in voluptuous waves. Borne on that wind, like the fragrance of salt upon a sea breeze, is a sweet scent, almost—but not quite—like the smell of a new-mown lawn. The aroma is rich and complex, an ethereal clue to the make-up of the vegetation that lies like an interwoven carpet design upon the face of the prairie—that is, in fact, the face of the prairie.

This unusual variety has long stimulated visitors. Walt Whitman, one of numerous poets and novelists who have rhapsodized on the West, was exhilarated by "every local sight and feature. Everywhere something characteristic—the cactuses, pinks, buffalo grass, wild sage."

The mosaic of grasses that flourish within the Dakota Badlands is particularly intricate and fascinating. For there the grasses and the very land itself occur within a set of subtle and diversified circumstances. The region is in a meteorological transition zone—and at a spot where elevation above sea level, combined with the climate, creates overlapping patterns in the vegetation.

A winding, shifting weatherman's line called the 16-inch isohyet—indicating the locale where 16 inches of annual rainfall occurs—wanders right through the middle of the Badlands. Across the face of the land stretching far off to either side of this line the grasses tend to differ—tall and succulent in the wetter east, short and hardy to the west. In addition, the elevation of land here has reached a rough average of about 1,400 feet in its slow climb from the Mississippi to the Rockies. And elevation, like the change in rainfall, exerts a force in the make-up of all the many ground plants.

Within the sweep of these continental influences are dozens of local factors—hills and valleys, northern and southern exposures, clayey and sandy soil, both virgin and disturbed earth—that contribute to the variety of the grassy plants. And over all, the sun and the seasons play their own powerful medley that brings change within change within change, contributing even further to the rich diversity of the mosaic, and to the elaborate life structure bound into each hardy leaf of grass.

A lush stand of tall prairie grass trembles under a passing gust of wind. The dominant growth in the area pictured here is common needle-and-thread grass, the most abundant species found in the Badlands prairie.

A turbulent spring thunderstorm explodes across the prairie, drenching the grass with the water that is its primary source of nourishment. The Badlands area receives about half of its annual rainfall in the period from April through June, much of it in sporadic thundershowers like this one.

Pioneers of the prairie, sunflowers take hold on badly eroded land, where the grass has died. Decomposing sunflowers help to rebuild

the land with fresh humus in which grass can grow again.

Roots of the white-blossomed field bindweed help to anchor prairie soil.

When a stretch of prairie nears maturity, scarlet globe mallow blooms.

Turning yellow as it begins to ripen, common needle-and-thread grass bows under the weight of its seeds. Needle-and-thread does its growing during the cool spring season, then takes on this autumnal appearance in June.

Curly buffalo grass and spearlike blue grama intertwine near the ground. Often found together, they are the most abundant short grasses in the so-called mixed-grass prairie, and can survive even in times of prolonged drought.

A needle-and-thread relative called green needle grass grows in characteristic bunches.

Tall sand reed grass reaches up from sandy soil—which its dense roots help to stabilize.

Bushy squirreltail grass, bowed over with

golden seeds, stands against a backdrop of Badlands sedimentary rock. This short, tufted grass prospers even in severely eroded soil.

Short grasses carpet the gentle pine-dotted slopes of an upland prairie in the cooler elevations of the approaches to the Black Hills. Where water collects in the shallow valleys, the grasses thrive, enlivening the landscape with deep slashes of dark, healthy green.

Ripe prairie asters offer their dried, fluffy autumn fruit to the wind, which will carry the countless seeds to new growing grounds.

Rich flowers decorate a prickly-pear cactus.

A bouquet of prairie violets mingles with yarrow, whose fernlike stems are not yet blooming.

Dainty pink blossoms adorn a meadow rose.

A gumbo lily—or evening-primrose—thrives in dry clay, drawing water from deep taproots.

An autumn moon glows over a panorama of upland prairie. Ponderosa pines like those scattered across this landscape become more

and more abundant as the altitude of the prairie increases. At 4,000 feet the grasses give way to trees, and prairie becomes woodland.

6/ An Untamable Terrain

*Nature has nowhere presented more beautiful and lovely
scenes, than those of the vast prairies of the West...
no nobler specimens than those who inhabit them — the
Indian and the buffalo — joint and original tenants
of the soil.* GEORGE CATLIN/ NORTH AMERICAN INDIANS

The Badlands have always attracted men by an arcane beauty that
never quite masks a hard reality: men can live in the Badlands only as
long as they live *with* the Badlands. Any attempt to remold this ca-
priciously carved terrain for human purposes is doomed to disaster.
"The industry of the settler will never succeed in cultivating and plant-
ing this fluctuating and sterile soil," wrote Father Pierre Jean De Smet,
a Jesuit missionary, after a visit in 1848. Thousands of years ago, Indians had reached a similar conclusion: the Badlands might be an
interesting place to visit—in the course of a hunt, perhaps—but nobody would want to stay there.

If nothing else, the swift and violent onset of the seasons, without
blend or meld, would be enough to warn of a wilderness that cannot be
controlled or mastered. Spring, with its inexorable floods, arrives in
late April, announced by heavy raindrops falling suddenly, warm on
the skin; it dies not many weeks later, a sigh in the night. Summer,
with its searing droughts, lasts somewhat longer. Autumn, like spring,
is short, a brief glow that fades before the keening winds and bitter
cold of a seemingly endless winter.

No one who has experienced the abruptness of the change of seasons in the Badlands is likely to forget it. I remember a night in early
June in my tent-camper near the White River. The evening had been
agreeable, with a cool breeze and isolated clouds in a serene, deep blue

sky. Canvas billowed gently around me as I fell asleep. At three in the morning I was awakened by a sharp gust that stretched into a despairing sob. When I awoke again a few hours later, the cool breeze of evening had given way to a pounding, parching wind, and my bedroll was soggy with sweat. Summer had come, and with it implacable heat and the unremitting westerly wind.

Autumn in the Badlands is also heralded by a sound: a change of tone in the rustle of the cottonwood leaves along the creek banks. The sound is sharp, crisp, agitated. By mid-September, the leaves take on the color of the morning sun—but the glory is short lived. Within days they fall and the branches of the twisted trees stand naked. Few flowers remain. Most of the survivors, though of admirable hardihood, bloom in unattractive shades of dusty yellow: noxious leafy spurge; curlycup gumweed, oozing a sticky fluid; malodorous prairie-dog weed; puncture vine, with half-inch spines that can flatten a bicycle tire.

The pace of animal life accelerates during this anxious interlude. All but a few year-round bird residents—like the black-billed magpie and the marsh hawk—head south, while such overwinterers as the slate-colored junco and tree sparrow move in. The bison calves in the Sage Creek Basin have grown to as much as 400 pounds from their spring birth weight of 25 to 40 pounds and have shed their tawny-red baby wool for the shaggy black winter coat of maturity. The prairie-dog towns are scenes of hustling, scurrying preparations for the onslaught of frost and freeze. There is much mending and expanding of burrows while the soil is still loose and workable. The spring pups have lost many of their playful ways and are as aggressive, if not as effective, as the adults in defending the town's boundaries against interlopers.

As the days grow chill and the nights long, the snake returns to the abandoned prairie-dog burrows from which it had been coaxed by springtime warmth. The jack rabbit's hind feet become heavily haired to serve as snowshoes; its buff pelt turns white for winter camouflage against marauding eagles and hawks. The striped skunk lines its den with grasses to ensure warmth and comfort during its fitful winter snoozing. The provident deer mouse hoards enough seeds in its burrow to last until spring, though it will occasionally emerge before then to nibble at seed heads protruding from the snow.

Finally and all too quickly, the Badlands autumn is over. I witnessed its abrupt demise, just as I had seen spring die; the end came on a night I like to recall as the Night of the Watery Moon. The day had been perfect: sunny, the temperature in the high 50s; only a few wisps of clouds threaded a bright blue sky. It was a day for walking, for breathing deeply, for pure enjoyment. I decided to work my leisurely way up the Cheyenne River from the little town of Wasta—relatively easy country. I had walked the Cheyenne downstream only a week before. That day had been raw, gusty and generally unpleasant, but I had seen numbers of small animals, a few deer and, everywhere, birds. Now, despite the magnificence of this day, I saw no animals among the thin line of trees along the river and, except for an occasional hawk high overhead, no birds. Aside from the sound of my breathing and the crunch of my boots on the dried clay of the riverbed, the stillness was absolute. I heard none of the mysterious whisperings that I had come to associate with the Badlands wilderness. For the first time that I could remember, there was not even the moan of the wind. In this silence, time lost dimension. Not until a blood-red sun began lowering and set the grassy Cheyenne River hills aflame, did I realize that it was time and past time to get back. As I hurried through the gathering darkness, the wind returned, chill and piercing. A moon appeared such as I had never seen before, a moon fit for witches to fly by, full but pale and —the only word that fits—watery.

That night, back in the town of Wall, I asked friends about this eerie moon. What, if anything, did it portend? To some, it meant snow was on the way; to others, a deep, killing frost. In either case, they agreed, the winter was going to be hard. Other omens were present. The woolly caterpillars' brown bands were abnormally wide; the ground squirrels had started seed collecting earlier than usual; the anthills were higher; the bark was thicker on the north side of the trees; the owls were hooting at midnight. Someone told me how to figure out how many times it would snow during the winter, using the formula of a bygone Sioux chief: "Take the day of the month of the first snow deep enough to track a cat, add the age of the moon, and that gives you the number of snows for the winter." Every Badlander has a tale of winter to tell—of frozen toes and fingers, of being lost in a blizzard, of pheasants starving because the grass is blanketed, of coyotes coming up to the doorstep begging for food. And so, though ours was a companionable group that night, there ran beneath the idle talk a thread of unease, a sense of bracing for the worst. No one thought to voice an essential truth about the Badlands—that this formidable and forbidding place is more suited for nomads than for settlers.

Many generations of people have passed through the Badlands,

The wintry face of the Badlands' Wall looms above the prairie, where snow accounts for less than 25 per cent of the area's precipitation.

paused and moved on. Nearly 50 prehistoric campsites have been discovered within Badlands National Monument, and more are nearby. Two sites were found just west of the monument in October 1970 by three rock hounds, who were searching for agates along the undercut banks of Bear Creek, south of the Cheyenne River. On a 26-foot-high white clay bank at a deep curve in the creek the men spotted two black smudges, one of them 10 feet and the other 20 feet above the creek. Recognizing an anomaly, they reported their find to the South Dakota School of Mines and Technology and to the South Dakota Geological Survey. A team of geologists was dispatched and quickly ascertained that the smudges were charcoal, remnants of long-extinct fires. Radiocarbon dating indicated that the charcoal in one smudge was more than 2,300 years old, in the other about 800 years old. The ancient hearths that once held the charcoal were only about two miles upstream from Bear Springs, an area used by Indians, fur traders and Army patrols for an overnight campsite as recently as the late 19th Century.

Excavation of the clay bank showed that the older of the two hearths had been 21 inches deep and 19 inches across. At the bottom of the fire pit, beneath the charcoal ash, the excavators found some fist-sized igneous rocks, whose presence puzzled the geologists. However, they found an explanation for this mystery. Such rocks had been swept from the Black Hills by streams and collected for use in a cooking technique that was undoubtedly first perfected by the prehistoric hunters and later adopted by the Sioux and other Plains Indians. A cooking pouch, made from a skin bag or the stomach of a bison, was filled with water and meat. Then the stones, which had been heated red hot in a fire pit, were picked up with a forked stick and dropped gently into the pouch. Almost immediately the water began boiling. The stew simmered for several days as the campers reheated the rocks, ate portions of the mess in the bag and added more meat. Finally, the pouch itself became tender and it, too, was eaten—an economy of resources hard to match.

One morning I walked along Bear Creek to the site of those old camps, but all traces of them had disappeared. A spring flood had undercut the clay bank and washed away the long-hidden evidence of human life that had been briefly revealed by an autumn rain. As I stood on the creek bed, looking at the place where the hearths had once glowed, I could not help feeling that some wisdom, some information had survived. I was reminded again that the parameters of life for man in the Badlands are narrow. A few things work well; many won't work at all.

Life here consists of conservation; waste is death. The survival skills of the band of hunters who had stopped at Bear Creek more than 2,000 years ago had worked well for them, and equally well just 100 years ago for the last nomads of this area—the Sioux.

Originally these wanderers had lived a more settled life in homes made of bark and earth, gathering berries, catching fish, and hunting animals on foot in the forests and lake country of the Mississippi River headwaters. Then, in the early 1700s, French fur traders started selling guns to the enemies of the Sioux, the Chippewa, who lived along the shores of Lake Superior. The Sioux tribes were forced out of the forests and moved westward up the Minnesota River Valley. Around 1775, one group, the Teton Sioux, finally crossed the Missouri to the prairie. During the decades of migration, the Teton Sioux themselves began to acquire firearms from the traders. More important, they learned from Western tribes such as the Arikara how to use horses.

The horse proved an indispensable ally to the Sioux in hunting elk, bison and even the fleet-footed pronghorn. On horseback the hunter could approach a herd and cut out and run down an animal that would otherwise be hard to stalk and harder to kill in open country. Dropping his single rein, the hunter would grasp his bow and five or six arrows in his left hand. In his right hand was a heavy quirt, or whip, fastened to the wrist by a thong. His horse, though well trained, was understandably reluctant to move too close to the horns of a thundering bison, but using quirt, knees and thighs the rider could maneuver his mount to the rear of a herd, then dash into its fringes and quickly isolate a straggler. Drawing closely alongside and to the right of his panting prey, he would set his arrow, draw the bow, lean forward and, as he neared the beast's shoulder, drive the shaft into its heart.

Even without the advantage of a mount, the hunter had other techniques he could use. In the winter, when the movement of animals was slowed by the deep, drifted snow, he sometimes hunted on snowshoes. And he learned to capitalize on the fact that bison, when in herds, have no fear of wolves. The hunter draped himself in a wolfskin and silently crept up on his prey, sometimes from a distance of half a mile; at the last instant, he stood and shot down the unsuspecting target.

The bison—*pte,* the Sioux called it—was the chief source of the Indians' ease and plenty, and the central factor of their life on the open grasslands. In cold weather the tribes broke up into small, family-based bands to live in sheltered sites along the tree-lined indentations of the creeks; in summer, when the flesh of the bison was fat and juicy, the bands came together for the first of two major hunts. If the kill was huge, the Sioux families feasted on the tongues and humps of the beasts; they dried the rest of the meat and used every other part of the animal.

In 1857 that astute observer of Indian life, the artist George Catlin, described the many uses to which the bison was put:

Every part of their flesh is converted into food, in one shape or another, and on it they (the Indians) entirely subsist. The robes of the animals are worn by the Indians instead of blankets—their skins when tanned, are used as coverings for their lodges, and for their beds; undressed, they are used for constructing canoes—for saddles, for bridles—l'arrêts (halters), lassos, and thongs. The horns are shaped into ladles and spoons—the brains are used for dressing the skins—their bones are used for saddle trees—for war clubs, and scrapers for graining the robes—and others are broken up for the marrow-fat which is contained in them. Their sinews are used for strings and backs to their bows—for thread to string their beads and sew their dresses. The feet of the animals are boiled, with their hoofs, for the glue they contain, for fastening their arrow points, and many other uses. The hair from the head and shoulders, which is long, is twisted and braided into halters, and the tail is used for a fly brush.

Catlin's breathless list, though long, was incomplete. The Indians also used the bison's thick neck skin for shields, its fat to produce that long-lasting trail food, pemmican, and its ribs to make runners for children's sleds. Intestines and bladder became containers for water. Finally, and not least, bison droppings were burned for fuel.

The Sioux were spectacularly successful in adapting to life in a new wilderness and in creating a culture as heavily dependent on a single undomesticated animal as were the early Northmen on the reindeer and the Eskimos on the seal. This self-contained and stringently tested system lasted only about 90 years. After white men began arriving in the West, the Sioux were never entirely free of the economy introduced by the newcomers. By the end of the 18th Century, fur traders roamed the upper Missouri prairie, exchanging firearms, pots, kettles and knives for buffalo hides and other skins. "Good White Man Came," reads the first entry in a 76-year chronicle kept by the chief of one Sioux band. In a set of pictographs painted on a roll of deerskin, the so-called winter count recorded the year's passing by noting its most important event. In the year 1807 a white man visited, shook hands, and brought food and gifts for all. The same scroll, when unrolled further, yields a poi-

Sioux hunters, one armed with a lance and the others with bow and arrow, close in on their buffalo quarry in this painting by George Catlin. To capture their own mounts—mustangs that once grazed among the buffalo— the Indians used lassos made of rawhide thongs. The same type of thong served as a halter; looped around the horse's lower jaw and trailing loosely, it could prevent the animal from escaping in case the rider fell off.

gnant history. In 1813 these Sioux saw their first firearm: the year of A Man with a Gun. The year 1818 is known simply as Smallpox—perhaps the white man's most unwelcome import—and so are the years 1845 and 1850. A quarter century later, 1876 is the year Went to Make a Treaty—the year the Sioux were forced to give up the Black Hills and all the area west of the great fork of the Cheyenne River.

As late as 1850, perhaps 40 million buffalo still roamed the Western plains. In 1873 the supply—and the slaughter—was so great that the price of a buffalo hide fell to 60 cents. General Philip Sheridan, an implacable enemy of the Indians, reported with satisfaction: "The Buffalo Hunters are destroying the Indians' commissary." By 1880, some 5,000 professional hunters and skinners were engaged in the slaughter. Driven to extremes, the Sioux resorted to an age-old mass-killing technique that they had used before, when the herds were numerous, but never with such devastating ecological impact. Arraying most of the tribe in two lines that formed a rough V, they would stampede an entire herd of bison between their ranks, converging at a cliff and driving the animals over the edge. Favorite spots for this activity were in the high bluffs over the White River; the flat river basin below made it easy to reach the carcasses.

Such pressure on the bison population compelled the Indians to accept an epochal compromise with their ancient way of life. In 1891, Commissioner of Indian Affairs T. J. Morgan wrote: "Within eight years from the agreement of 1876 the buffalo had gone, and the Sioux had left to them alkali land and government rations. . . . Suddenly, almost without warning, they were expected at once and without previous training to settle down to the pursuits of agriculture in a land largely unfitted for such use. The freedom of the chase was to be exchanged for the idleness of the camp." A hunting economy essentially in balance with the resources of the area was to be discarded for an agrarian culture dependent on the whims of weather. The Indians had lived successfully *with* the Badlands; when forced to try to live *on* them, as the white man thought they could, the Indians failed.

The Sioux were unaware of Commissioner Morgan's dire report. A year earlier, in the spring of 1890, they had received word of impending salvation from a visionary, a Paiute shepherd named Wovoka. When spring rolled around again, according to Wovoka, deer, antelope, elk and buffalo herds would roam a lush, new grassland in abundance, and they and the Indians would enjoy eternal life. God had sent him, Wovoka said, to "renew everything as it used to be and make it better." All

the Indians had to do was to sing the songs of the Ghost Dance ceremony: by praying and dancing, they could "die"—fall on the ground in
a hypnotic trance—and be transported briefly to the new earth even before it arrived.

Alluring as the prospect was, the Sioux did not attempt to perform
the Ghost Dance until one siege of especially bad weather forcefully sig-
naled that the Badlands would not accept them as farmers and
homesteaders. Pressured by the federal agents, made desperate by cuts
in government rations of beef, the Sioux had tried to plant gardens in
the grassland. But in mid-July of 1890, scorching westerly winds swept
across the plains, continuing relentlessly throughout the summer. The
pitiful gardens died; starvation began killing the old, newborn and sick.
In August the Ghost Dance began.

By late autumn, thousands of Sioux in and around the Badlands were
caught up by the dance. They brought their children to the ceremonies,
which went on day and night. Missionaries and white teachers whose
classes had disappeared joined Indian agents and United States Army
officers first in pleas, then in demands, that the dancing stop. On November 15, the inexperienced Indian agent at Pine Ridge Indian
Reservation, Daniel F. Royer, wired the Acting Commissioner of Indian Affairs: "Indians are dancing in the snow and are wild and crazy.
. . . We need protection and we need it now. . . . Nothing short of
1,000 soldiers will settle this dancing." By November 20, columns
of troops began arriving to keep an eye on the dancers.

The Sioux chiefs and medicine men who led the dances were alarmed.
Word went out to the various bands, and by November 30 some 600
Sioux warriors gathered on the banks of the White River, marched
north and climbed the steep slopes of Cuny Table. They crossed the table to the northeast edge, where a land bridge—scarcely wide enough
for a wagon—led to a triangular peninsula about three miles long and
two miles wide. The Sioux faithful called this place the Stronghold.
Here, through late November and into December, they danced to hasten
the return of spring and the new land and buffalo promised by Wovoka.

In mid-December the tensions aroused by the Ghost Dance craze ex-
ploded into violence and bloodshed. From his camp at Standing Rock
Reservation, north of Pine Ridge, the great chief Sitting Bull was en-
couraging the continuation of the dancing. Special police under orders
from Fort Yates, the military post on the reservation, arrived to arrest
Sitting Bull and in the resulting scuffle he was killed. From that moment,

with greater tragedy yet to come, the Ghost Dance fever ebbed. As the days passed, groups of dancers were lured from the Stronghold by promises of clemency. Late in December, two chiefs, Kicking Bear and Short Bull, led the last of the hard-core dancers down from the plateau.

At the same time, some 350 Sioux men, women and children under Chief Big Foot were trekking south into Pine Ridge Indian Reservation at the invitation of several tribal factions who wanted Big Foot to adjudicate some disputes. The military misunderstood Big Foot's intentions and intercepted the band near Wounded Knee Creek. The next morning, United States Army officers demanded that the Indians surrender their rifles. A surrender began—with both sides tense, fearful and itchy fingered. A gun went off accidentally and in seconds the Indians and the nearly 500 blue-coated soldiers were firing everything they had at each other. Some Indians escaped, but Big Foot and at least 152 others died, many of them women and children. The Army lost 25.

For the Sioux, the chief result of this final defeat was that white settlers pressed in ever closer around the Badlands. Despite the adverse reports on the exploitable possibilities of the area by practically every rational observer of the preceding century, despite the forbidding climate and terrain, some whites clung to the notion that somehow the Badlands area could be made to pay. A theory persisted that it was underlaid by a vast bed of coal that spontaneous combustion had converted into oil. There was hope that gold might be found, as in the Black Hills, or that the Badlands might contain other valuable minerals.

Land speculators thrived in the new towns that had sprung up along the railroad tracks crossing the Badlands. Recruiters went as far abroad as Russia to persuade settlers that South Dakota could produce just about every crop under the sun. The Badlands did not welcome the new arrivals. Of those who came and struggled, many more moved on than stayed. The harsh drought of 1911, when grasshoppers ravaged the spindly crops, drove large numbers of settlers away. The population of the area actually declined sharply for a few years, only to pick up again with the hopes engendered by the high price that grain fetched during the First World War.

These bright hopes died in the drought of the 1930s, the Dust Bowl years, when the very land blew out from under men's boots. Homestead after homestead, officially classified by the government as submarginal for farming, was abandoned or sold to the government for as little as three dollars an acre.

The calamity gave impetus to a movement to save at least a portion of the threatened wilderness by making it a national park or monument. To some people, the very thought had long been ridiculous. John Burroughs, the great naturalist, had characterized the Badlands in 1903 as "utterly demoralized and gone to the bad . . . flayed, fantastic, treeless, a riot of naked clay slopes, chimney-like buttes and dry coulees." Artists, most of them blinkered by 19th Century standards of natural beauty, had generally avoided the Badlands. "They are somewhat as Doré pictured Hell," said the painter Frederic Remington. "One set of buttes, with cones and minarets, gives place in the next mile to natural freaks of a different variety, never dreamed of by mortal man."

Yet, after decades of political maneuvering and bureaucratic papershuffling, in 1939 Badlands National Monument was established. Within the invisible wall of government protection, the blue grama, the buffalo grass and the little bluestem that had nourished the buffalo herds crept back. A few at a time, birds and many of the small animals returned. The nation had found the limits to its defiance of the Badlands and acknowledged them.

I had one last reminder of the land's harshness on the morning after the Night of the Watery Moon. Beneath a sun that shone without warming, the land was transformed. Mile after mile, every stem and every blade of grass, every branch and every twig of tree and bush was covered by a quarter inch of glittering, blinding frost. Small birds shook off crystal jewels with every wingbeat. From yesterday's clemencies, the temperature had dropped to 8° F. And out of the north rang the metallic percussion of winter thunder.

June in the North

PHOTOGRAPHS BY STEVEN C. WILSON

The Badlands of North Dakota, like those to the south, are a panorama of bare, broken, eroded rocks and other distinctive land forms. Yet during the early summer these northern Badlands can come to life as a misty, surrealistic realm of lush river valleys and green upland prairies.

That is the way photographer Steve Wilson found the area when he arrived in June after a drenching May in which seven inches of rain had fallen—nearly half the normal total for a whole year. To record the vivid contrasts between crumbling erosion and the blooming grassland, Wilson spent a week at Theodore Roosevelt National Memorial Park, a spread of 70,000 acres where Roosevelt once raised cattle and lived the life of a cowboy.

Wilson discovered to his fascination that while parching, dry winds waft overhead in June, the lowlands are often heavy with humidity. "You feel there are invisible walls of water in the air squeezing you in," he noted. The main source of this high humidity is the Little Missouri River, the largest watercourse in either of the Dakotas' Badlands.

Full-flowing in early summer, the river nourishes thick growths of cottonwoods and willows. Furthermore, the river's waters are evaporated by hot prairie sun throughout the long days; and when night cools the air, the moisture condenses into heavy mist. By morning, thick banks of ground fog develop: at dawn one day, Wilson walked into a fog bank he calculated as being 800 feet thick.

In this land of contrasts, a diversity of other sights caught Wilson's eye: the solemnity of an ancient tree stump—probably a sequoia—buried by volcanic ash 60 million years ago, and petrified; a bank of wallflower nodding in the breeze; a blue mass of a clay called bentonite that oozes and flows when wet.

Under the blaze of the midday sun Wilson put away his cameras, having discovered that the land forms became bleached and flattened by the severe light. The magical hours for photography were sunup and sunset. Then, in the oblique rays, he found "the emotional communication of light as it reacts or reflects on physical things."

At such times, meandering past stands of barren rock, plateaus of grassland and foggy, watery lowlands, Wilson experienced the same moods of excitement and tranquillity that must have stirred Teddy Roosevelt nearly a century before.

SANDSTONE BLOCKS SPLIT BY FROST

FLUTED WEATHERING IN A BANK OF SILTSTONE

A PETRIFIED TREE STUMP

PATTERNS OF EROSION

SUNSET AT A BEND IN THE LITTLE MISSOURI

A SLOPE OF WALLFLOWER

HILLS AND HUMMOCKS OF CLAY

SAND RIPPLES ON A DRY STRETCH OF THE LITTLE MISSOURI BED

ALKALI STREAKS ON THE BOTTOM OF APPEL CREEK

LINGERING FOG IN THE LOWLANDS

BIBLIOGRAPHY

*Also available in paperback.
†Available in paperback only.

Allen, Durward L., *The Life of Prairies and Plains.* McGraw-Hill, 1967.

†Bent, Arthur Cleveland, *Life Histories of North American Birds of Prey,* Parts I and II. Dover Publications, 1961.

†Bormann, Ernest G., *Homesteading in the Badlands—1912.* Privately printed, 1971.

†Brooks, Chester L., and Ray H. Mattison, *Theodore Roosevelt and the Dakota Badlands.* National Park Service, 1958.

Brown, Leslie, and Dean Amadon, *Eagles, Hawks and Falcons of the World,* 2 vols. McGraw-Hill, 1968.

†Busch, Noel F., *T. R.* Apollo Editions, 1963.

Cahalane, Victor H., *Mammals of North America.* Macmillan, 1947.

Clark, John, *Oligocene Drainages in the Big Badlands of South Dakota.* 1962.

Clark, John, J. R. Beerbower and K. K. Kietzke, *Oligocene Sedimentation, Stratigraphy, Paleoecology and Paleoclimatology in the Big Badlands of South Dakota.* Field Museum of Natural History, 1967.

Costello, David F., *The World of the Prairie Dog.* J. B. Lippincott, 1970.

Drimmer, Frederick, Editor-in-Chief, *The Animal Kingdom,* 2 vols. Doubleday, 1954.

Gilliard, E. Thomas, *Living Birds of the World.* Doubleday, 1958.

Grzimek, Bernard, *Grzimek's Animal Life Encyclopedia.* Van Nostrand Reinhold, 1972.

Hagedorn, Hermann, *Roosevelt in the Badlands.* Houghton Mifflin, 1921.

†Harksen, J. C., and J. R. Macdonald, *Guidebook to the Major Cenozoic Deposits of Southwestern South Dakota.* Guidebook 2, South Dakota Geological Survey, Science Center, University of South Dakota, 1969.

†Hauk, Joy Keve, *Badlands: Its Life and Landscape.* Badlands Natural History Association, 1969.

Klauber, Laurence M., *Rattlesnakes,* Vol. I. University of California Press, 1956.

Lorant, Stefan, *The Life and Times of Theodore Roosevelt.* Doubleday, 1959.

*Mooney, James, *The Ghost-Dance Religion and the Sioux Outbreak of 1890,* Anthony F. C. Wallace, ed. University of Chicago Press, 1965.

†Neihardt, John G., *Black Elk Speaks.* Pocket Books, 1972.

Orr, Robert T., *Mammals of North America.* Doubleday, 1971.

Palmer, Ralph S., *The Mammal Guide.* Doubleday, 1954.

Pasture and Range Plants. Phillips Petroleum Co., 1963.

Pearson, T. Gilbert, *Birds of America.* Garden City Publishing Co., 1936.

Pough, Richard H., *Audubon Western Guide.* Doubleday, 1957.

†Pringle, Henry F., *Theodore Roosevelt: A Biography.* Harcourt Brace Jovanovich, 1956.

Rand, Austin L., *Birds of North America.* Doubleday, 1971.

*Robbins, Chandler S., Bertel Bruun and Herbert S. Zim, *Birds of North America.* Western Publishing Company, 1966.

Romer, Alfred Sherwood, *Vertebrate Paleontology.* University of Chicago Press, 3rd ed., 1966.

Roosevelt, Theodore, *Theodore Roosevelt, an Autobiography.* Charles Scribner's Sons, 1946.

†Theodore Roosevelt Centennial Commission, *A Compilation on the Life and Career of Theodore Roosevelt.* U.S. Govt. Printing Office, 1958.

Schmidt, Karl P., and D. Dwight Davis, *Field Book of Snakes of the United States and Canada.* G. P. Putnam's Sons, 1941.

Sears, Paul B., *Lands beyond the Forest.* Prentice-Hall, 1969.

Stebbins, Robert C., *A Field Guide to Western Reptiles and Amphibians.* Houghton Mifflin, 1966.

Sunder, John E., *The Fur Trade on the Upper Missouri 1840-1865.* University of Oklahoma Press, 1965.

†Swartzlow, Carl R., and Robert F. Upton, *Badlands National Monument, South Dakota.* Natural History Handbook Series No. 2, 1954.

*Utley, Robert M., *The Last Days of the Sioux Nation.* Yale University Press, 1963.

†Van Bruggen, Theodore, *Wildflowers of the Northern Plains and Black Hills.* Badlands Natural History Association, 1971.

Wright, Albert Hazen and Anna Allen, *Handbook of Snakes of the United States and Canada,* Vol. II. Comstock Publishing Associates, 1957.

Periodicals and Articles

Borchert, John R., "The Climate of the Central North American Grassland." *Annals of the Association of American Geographers,* March 1950.

King, John A., "The Social Behavior of Prairie Dogs." *Scientific American,* October 1959.

O'Harra, Cleophas C., *The White River Badlands.* Bulletin No. 13, Dept. of Geology, South Dakota School of Mines and Technology, 1920.

Witzke, Brian, "The Badlands and Their Fossils." *Earth Science,* November-December 1972.

Acknowledgments

The author and editors of this book are particularly indebted to Sidney S. Horenstein, Department of Invertebrate Paleontology, The American Museum of Natural History, New York City; and Theodore Van Bruggen, Professor of Biology, University of South Dakota, Vermillion, South Dakota. They also wish to thank the following persons and institutions. In Chicago: John G. Cawelti, Professor of English and Humanities, University of Chicago; John Clark, Field Museum of Natural History; Robert Hall, Professor of Anthropology, University of Illinois at Chicago Circle Campus. In Kansas: E. Raymond Hall, University of Kansas, Museum of Natural History, Lawrence; F. Robert Henderson, Cooperative Extension Service, Kansas State University, Manhattan. In Massachusetts: Wallace Finley Dailey, Curator, Theodore Roosevelt Collection, Harvard College Library, Cambridge. In Michigan: John A. King, Professor of Zoology, Michigan State University, East Lansing. In New York: John A. Gable, Executive Director, Theodore Roosevelt Association, Oyster Bay. In New York City: Charles R. Long, The New York Botanical Garden; John Behler, Associate Curator of Herpetology, Joseph L. Bell, Curator of Ornithology, Donald F. Bruning, Associate Curator of Ornithology, James G. Doherty, Associate Curator of Mammals, New York Zoological Park. In North Dakota: Wilford L. Miller, Bismarck; John O. Lancaster, John Muller, Bob Pell, Hank Schock, Bill Wellman, Theodore Roosevelt National Memorial Park, Medora; Theodore Roosevelt Nature and History Association, Medora; Russ Hanson, Gary Leppert, Joseph A. Satrom, North Dakota Highway Department, Bismarck; Rikki Thompson, Bismarck; Frank E. Vyzralek, State Historical Society of North Dakota, Bismarck. In South Dakota: Larry Hannoman, Carol Johnston, Russell B. King, Cecil D. Lewis Jr., Shirley Norton, Paul L. Swearingen, James G. Wilson, Badlands National Monument, Interior; Badlands Natural History Association, Interior; Kenneth D. Renner, Donald W. Schmidtlein, Buffalo Gap National Grassland, Wall; Linda Hughes, South Dakota Department of Economic and Tourism Development, Pierre; Dayton W. Canaday, Janice Fleming, Historical Resource Center, South Dakota Department of Education and Cultural Affairs, Pierre; J. C. Harksen, South Dakota Geological Survey, Rapid City; Joy Keve Hauk, Cottonwood; Max and Nancy Hauk, Wall; Conrad Hillman, U.S. Bureau of Sport Fisheries and Wildlife, Rapid City; Leonel Jensen, Wall; Lane Johnston, Interior; Clarence Jurisch, Scenic; Raymond Linder, South Dakota Cooperative Wildlife Research Unit, South Dakota State University, Brookings; Tal Lockwood, Custer State Park, Hermosa; Lyle O'Rourke, Interior; Robert W. Wilson, Professor of Geology, South Dakota School of Mines and Technology, Rapid City; Joe Allen, Thomas M. Bean, Alan Lovaas, Lester F. McClanahan, Jack O'Brien, Wind Cave National Park, Hot Springs. In Washington, D.C.: Tom Garrett, Friends of the Earth. In Wisconsin: Tim W. Clark, Department of Zoology, University of Wisconsin, Madison. In Wyoming: Susan J. Sindt, Yellowstone National Park.

Picture Credits

Sources for the pictures in this book are shown below. Credits for pictures from left to right are separated by semicolons; from top to bottom they are separated by dashes.

Cover—Enrico Ferorelli. End papers 2, 3, 4, page 1, 2, 3—Enrico Ferorelli. 4, 5—Jim Brandenburg. 6, 7—Enrico Ferorelli. 8, 9—Steven C. Wilson. 10 through 13—Enrico Ferorelli. 18—Maps produced by Hunting Surveys Limited. 22, 23—Enrico Ferorelli. 25—Steven C. Wilson. 30, 31—Jim Brandenburg. 34, 35—Theodore Roosevelt Collection, Harvard College Library. 36, 37—Theodore Roosevelt, Theodore Roosevelt Collection, Harvard College Library. 38, 39—Theodore Roosevelt, Theodore Roosevelt Collection, Harvard College Library; Theodore Roosevelt Collection, Harvard College Library. 40, 41—Theodore Roosevelt, Theodore Roosevelt Collection, Harvard College Library; Underwood and Underwood. 45—Enrico Ferorelli. 49—Sid Horenstein. 50, 51—Jim Brandenburg. 55 through 69—Enrico Ferorelli. 72—Enrico Ferorelli. 76, 77—Enrico Ferorelli. 78—Richard Erdoes. 82 through 93—David Cavagnaro. 96, 97—Jim Brandenburg. 100, 101—Glenn D. Chambers; Richard Erdoes—Jim Brandenburg—B. J. Rose. 104 through 123—Jim Brandenburg. 126—Jim Brandenburg. 130, 131—Enrico Ferorelli. 132—David Cavagnaro. 134—Enrico Ferorelli. 139 through 153—Enrico Ferorelli. 156, 157—John W. Stockert. 161—George Catlin, courtesy of National Collection of Fine Arts, Smithsonian Institution. 167 through 179—Steven C. Wilson.

Index

Numerals in italics indicate a photograph or drawing of the subject mentioned.

A

Agate(s), *52, 89, 158*
Alkali, *177*
Ammonite, *78*
Animals, 94-96, 98-99, *100-101,* 102-104, 106-107, 165; prehistoric, 44, 46, 48, 50, 71, 73, 74, 75, *77, 78, 79-81. See also* specific types
Antelope. *See* Pronghorn
Anthills, 156; and fossils, 73-74
Ants: harvester, 73-74; stick mound, *91*
Aphids, *91*
Apple Creek, *177*
Aspen, 86, 125
Asters, prairie, *150*

B

Bad River, 21, 22
Badger(s) *(Taxidea taxus), 101,* 133
Badlands: climate, 29-30, 32-33, 54, 133; climatic changes, 47-48, 50, 72, 79; formation, *20-23,* 33, 54, *58-59, 64-65 (see also* Erosion); general description, 20-22, 24, 26-29, 33; geological history, 42-44, 46-48, 50-52; Great Wall, 18, 26, 28, 30, 43, 50, 74, 127, 137, *156-157;* in Indian lore, 21; land speculators in, 164; *map 18-19;* as meteorological transition zone, 138; Oligocene epoch, 71, 72, 73, 79; prehistoric campsites, 158-159; river systems, 21-22; seasons, 154-155; settlers and homesteaders in, 16, 24, 132, 164; terrain, *cover, end paper 2-page 9, 12-13, 22-23, 24, 31, 55, 60-61, 66, 68-69, 76-77, 130-131, 147, 148-149, 152-153, 174-175, 178-179. See also* Big Badlands; North Dakota Badlands; South Dakota Badlands
Badlands National Monument (South Dakota), *cover, map* 18, 28, 70, 94, 102, 106, 165
Bear(s), 102; grizzly, 103
Bear Creek, 158, 159
Bee(s): burrows, *84;* solitary, *84*

Beggar's-tick, 86
Big Badlands (South Dakota), 21, 138
Bigfoot Pass, *6-7*
Bindweed, field *(Convolvus arvensis), 143*
Birds, 94, 165; seed transportation by, 83, 135. *See also* specific types
Bison, or buffalo *(Bison bison bison),* 94, 102, 103-104, 135; bones, *84;* calves, 155; destruction of, 84, 102-103; and Indians, 159-160, *161,* 162; original herds, 125, 162; and prairie dogs, *118,* 119; and prairie grass, 133; and Theodore Roosevelt, 34
Black Hills, 21, 47, 50, 52, 71, 72, 78, 89, 128, *148-149,* 158, 162, 164; formation of, 46
Blazing star *(Liatris squarrosa),* 137
Bobcat(s), 85, 102
Bouncing Bet, 136
Box elder bug *(Leptocoris trivittatus), 91*
Buffalo. *See* Bison
Buffalo, wood *(Bison bison athabascae),* 102-103
Buffalo bur, 136
Buffaloberry, 86, 103, 127
Bulrush(es), 86
Burns Basin, *130-131*
Burroughs, John, quoted, 165

C

Cactus, 138, *151;* prickly-pear *(Opuntia polyacantha), 89,* 104, *134,* 137
Camel(s), 71, 75; evolution of, 80
Castle Butte, *cover*
Caterpillar(s): eastern tent *(Malacosoma americana), 92;* hairy, *91*
Cather, Willa, quoted, 127
Catlin, George: painting by, *161;* quoted, 103, 154, 160
Cavagnaro, David, 82, 87
Cedar (juniper), 90, 92
Cedar Pass, *2-3,* 95
Chadron Formation, 48, 50
Chert, 47
Cheyenne River, 22, 70, 98, 132, 156, 158, 162
Chipmunk(s), 27; Black Hills, or Badlands, 100

Chokecherry, 86, 92
Clark, John, 46
Clay, 30, 47, *50-51,* 60, 62, *64-65, 67, 134, 151, 174-175;* bentonite, 166
Clover, sweet, 104
Cocklebur *(Xanthum strumarium),* 83; seeds, *83*
Cottonwood(s), 20, 30, 33, 127, 155, 166; *(Populus deltoides), 84-85*
Cottonwood Creek, 81
Coyote *(Canis latrans),* 82, *101,* 156; pup, *112-113*
Coyote Creek, 82, 84, *85,* 86; mouth, *82-83*
Creeping Jenny, 136
Culbertson, Thaddeus, quoted, 29

D

Dandelion, 92
De Smet, Father Pierre Jean, quoted, 27, 154
Deer, 82, 155, 162; mule, 102; white-tailed, 106
Dogwood, red osier, 86

E

Elk, 16, 102, 125, 159
Elm, American *(Ulmus americana),* 86; bark, *86*
Elsevier geologic time scale, 27
Erosion: of cultivated soil, 132-133; by frost, 31, *167;* grass-to-grass cycle, *58-59;* and rock formations, *4-5, 8-9,* 30, 42, 44, *60-61, 62, 63, 170-171;* by water, 33, *49,* 52, 54, 57, 58, 60, 62, *64-65, 66, 67;* by weathering, 47, 131, *168;* by wind, *66*

F

Feldspar, 47
Ferorelli, Enrico, 107
Ferret, black-footed *(Mustela nigripes), 101,* 102
Flax, Russian, 136
Flooding and floodplains, 24, 30, 32, 45-46, 47, 50, 85, *93,* 154
Flowers, 136-137, 155, 165; prairie, 138, *142-143, 150-151. See also* specific types
Fossils and fossilization, 42, *72,* 73; animal, 70, 71, 72-74, *76-77, 78, 79-81;*

collecting expeditions, 74-75, 78; seed, 74
Frog(s), 87; leopard (Rana pipiens), 87

G
Garnet, 52
Geologic time scale, 27
Goldenrod (Solidago missouriensis), 132
Grackle(s), 94-96, 99; bronze, 95
Grass(es), 6-7, 27, 52, 58; blue grama (Bouteloua gracilis), 129, 130-131, 132, 133, 135, 145, 165; bluestem, short (Andropógon scoparius), 125, 127, 129, 130-131, 135, 165; buffalo (Buchloë dactyloides), 129, 132, 133, 138, 145, 165; Canada wild rye, 127; desiccation resistance, 127, 129, 132; and drought, 133, 135, 145; and ecological balance, 133, 135; and erosion cycle, 58-59; evolution of, 128-129; fertilization of, 129; green needle (Stipa virigila), 146; Indian, 125; "invader," 133, 135-136; Japanese brome, 135; needle-and-thread (Stipa comata), 125, 128, 138, 144-145; and other plants, 135-137; porcupine (see Grass(es), needle-and-thread); prairie, 6-7, 139; rabbit-foot, 135; sand dropseed, 127; sand reed (Calamovilfa longifolia), 90, 146; and seed dispersal, 129, 135; and soil conservation, 124-125, 146; squirreltail (Sitanion bystrix), 146-147; Stonyhill muhly, 135; western wheat, 128, 129
Grasshopper(s), 100; plague (1911), 164
Grasslands. See Prairie
Grouse, sharp-tailed, 96, 98, 100
Gumbo, 70; slope, 88, 89
Gumbo lily (Oenothera caesipatos), 89, 137, 151
Gumweed, curlycup, 155

H
Hackberry, 74, 86
Hauk, Max, 80-81, 82, 85, 87, 92
Hauk, Nancy, 89, 91
Hawk(s), 95, 106-107, 156; marsh, 155
Hay Butte, 22-23
Hayden, Ferdinand V., 75, 78, 87; quoted, 70

Horse(s), 71, 80; evolution of, 78-79; and Indians, 159; three-toed fossil, 128

I
Imlay (South Dakota), 52, 124-125
Indians, 21, 39, 43, 71, 80, 132, 154, 161, 163; Arikara, 159; and bison, 160, 161, 162; campsites, 158-159; Chippewa, 159; conflict with whites, 103, 132, 160, 163-164; Dakota, 21; Ghost Dance ceremony, 163-164; and horses, 159-160, 161; hunting techniques, 159-160, 161, 162; Paiute, 162; Plains, 158. See also Sioux Indians
Ingalls, Senator James, quoted, 124
Irving, Washington, quoted, 125

J
Jasper, 47, 52
Johnston, Lane, 82, 85, 92
Johnston, Midge, 91
Junco, slate-colored, 155

K
Kicking Bear, Chief, 164
Killdeer, 98
Kulp geologic time scale, 27

L
Lewis, Meriwether, quoted, 125
Limestone, 47, 48
Little Missouri River, 18, 25, 37, 166, 172, 176
Lizards, 94; sagebrush, 89
Logston Spring Marsh, 86, 87

M
Magpie, 100; black-billed, 155
Mallow, globe (Sphaeralcea coccinea), 143
Marshes, 86, 87
Meadowlark, western (Sturnella neglecta), 90, 91, 92, 126
Mesquite, 133
Minerals, 46, 49, 50, 55, 164. See also specific types
Missouri River, 21, 22, 43, 44, 52, 78, 125, 135
Mountain lion, 102
Mouse, 94; deer, 155; grasshopper, 100
Mudstone, 52, 54, 55, 62

N
Norbeck Pass, 12-13
North Dakota Badlands, 28, 138, 166

O
O'Harra, Cleophas C., quoted, 42
Oligocene epoch, 71-73, 79
Onions, textile (Allium textile), 89
Owl(s), 156; burrowing (Speotyto cunicularia), 102, 105

P
Paintbrush, Indian (Castilleja sessiliflora), 91
Parsnip, water, 86
Penstemon (Penstemon angustifolius), 91; shell-leafed (Penstemon grandiflorus), 126
Petrified wood, 89, 169
Pine, ponderosa (Pinus ponderosa), 152-153
Pine Ridge Indian Reservation, 82, 95, 163, 164
Pinks, 138
Plum, wild, 86, 127
Porcupine(s), 82, 85, 86
Prairie, 94, 124-125, 127-129, 133-135, 138, 139, 140-141; annual precipitation, 140; and cattle-grazing, 132; climax grassland, 133; flowers, 138, 142-143, 150-151; homesteaders, 132, 133; mixed-grass, 145; seasonal variations, 138, 140, 145; upland, 148-149, 152-153. See also Grass(es)
Prairie dog(s), black-tailed (Cynomys ludovicianus), 108, 109-123, 133, 155; and bison, 118, 119; burrow networks, 108, 119; coterie organization, 108, 115; feeding habits, 114, 115, 116, 119; grooming behavior, 116, 117; hibernation, 115; kissing gesture, 110, 116; migration, 115; mountain species, 115; and predators, 108, 112, 113; pups, 116, 117, 120, 121, 122-123, 155; territorial defense behavior, 109, 111, 112, 113; warning calls and positions, 109, 112, 113
Prickly pear. See Cactus
Pronghorn(s) (Antilocapra americana), 97, 104, 106, 125, 133, 159, 160
Puncture vine, 155

Q

Quartz, 47, 52

R

Rabbit(s), 82; cottontail, 91; jack, 106, 155
Ranching, cattle, *38-39*, 132; and animal populations, 102
Red admiral *(Vanessa atalanta)*, *92*
Red River, 47, 72
Red River Valley, 46, 47, 48
Red-winged blackbird *(Agelaius phoenicus)*, 24; nest, *87*
Remington, Frederic, quoted, 165
Rock: sedimentary, 44, *45*, 52, *147*; striated, 46, *49*, *50*, *55*
Rock formations, 26, *63*, 67, 82, *167*, *168*, *170-171*; buttes, *22-23*; "carrot stick," 53; cliffs, *49*; dikes, *62*; faults, 46; mounds, 46, 47, *50-51*, *64-65*, *90*; plateaus, *8-9*; ridges, 46; slumps, *68-69*, 82, *90*; terraces, 58. *See also* Badlands, terrain
Rocky Mountains, 21, 47, 53, 72
Roosevelt, Franklin D., 135
Roosevelt, Theodore, 18, 21, 34, *35*, 39, 166; Elkhorn Ranch, 34, *36*, *37*; and Maltese Cross Ranch, 34, *38*, *39*; national parks, monuments and reserves legacy, 34; photographs by, *36*, *37*, *38*, *40*; quoted, 39
Rose, meadow *(Rosa arkansana)*, 127, *151*
Rose, wild *(Rosa blanda)*, 132

S

Sabertooth cat, 80
Sackett, Charles, quoted, 94
Sage, 27, 89; wild, 138
Sage Creek, 42, 43, 44, 46, *49*, 70, 81, 102, 106
Sage Creek Basin, *22-23*, 43, 100, 155
Sagebrush, 125, 133
Sagewort, cudweed, 104
Salamander, tiger, 99
Salsify, western *(Tragopogon porrifolius)*, *10-11*
Saltbush, *4-5*
Sandstone, 47, 54, *66-67*, 167
Sedge, carex *(Carex haydenii)*, 87
Shale, *end paper 4-page 1*, 33, 43-44, *45*,

48, 54, 86; Pierre, 44, 46, *49*, 50, 71
Sheep: Audubon bighorn, 60, 102; Rocky Mountain bighorn, 102
Sheep Mountain Table, 42, 47, 50, 52, *60-61*, *79*, 124
Sheridan, General Philip, quoted, 162
Short Bull, Chief, 164
Siderite, *45*
Siltstone, 54, *55*, *62*, 168
Sioux Indians, 16, 71; and bison, 159-160, *161*; campsites, 158; conflict with whites, 78, 163-164; Oglala, 52-53; sayings, 156; Teton, 159
Sitting Bull, Chief, 163
Skunk, striped, 155
Snake(s), 94, 102, 155; bull *(Pituophis melanoleucus)*, 101; hognose, 98-99, 100; plains garter, 106; puff adder, 98; rattlesnakes, 99
Soapweed, 137
Sod, *50-51*, *59*; formation of, 129; houses, 132; tables, *22-23*, 124
South Dakota Badlands, 20, 138
Sparrow, tree, 155
Spider, black-widow, 91
Spring(s), formation, 86-87
Spring-azure butterfly, 82
Spruce, 125
Spurge, leafy, 155
Squirrel, ground, 156
Standing Rock Reservation, 163
Striation, mineral, *49*, *50*, *55*
Sunflower(s) *(Helicanthus annuus)*, *142-143*
Swallows, cliff, 27, 95; and grackles, 95-96; nests, *84*, 95

T

Tennyson, Lord Alfred, quoted, 90
Theodore Roosevelt National Memorial Park, 28-29, 34, 106, 166
Thistle, Russian, 136
Titanothere, 71, 73, 74, 75, 81
Toad(s): Great Plains, 89; spadefoot, 99
Toadflax, bastard *(Comandra umbellata)*, 89
Tourmaline, 52
Traders, fur, 16, 21, 43, 74, 158, 159, 160
Tumbleweed, 136
Turtle(s), 70, 71, 75, *77*

U

U.S. Army, 78, 80, 163, 164
U.S. Army Corps of Engineers, 135
U.S. Congress, homestead legislation (1889), 132
U.S. Forest Service, 135

V

Van Bruggen, Theodore, 84, 86, 89, 91, 135
Violets, prairie *(Viola pedatifida)*, *151*
Volcanic ash, 47, 50, *50-51*, 53, *63*, 166
Vulture Peak, *30-31*

W

Wallflower, western *(Erysimum asperum)*, 91, 166, *173*
Weather: drought, 133, 135, 145, 154, 163, 164; fog, *25*, 166, *178-179*; frost, 167; humidity, 166; rainfall, 24, 29-30, 32-33, *64-65*, 67, 138, 140, 166; seasonal change, 154-156; snow, *156-157*; storms, 30, *31*, *32-33*, 93, *140-141*; thunderhead, *end paper 4-page 1*; western wind, 22, 24, 27, 29, 54. *See also* Erosion
Weed(s), 136; prairie-dog, 155; water, 86
White River, 20, 21, *22*, 28, 30, 32, 50, *56-57*, 70, 78, 82, 86, 92, 93, 95, 127, 130-131, 163; floodplain, 32, *93*; tributaries, *62*, 131
White River Basin, 26, 52, 124
Whitman, Walt, quoted, 138
Willow, 166; peach-leafed, 86
Wilson, Jim, 104
Wilson, Steve, 166
Wind: erosion, *66*; and seed transportation, 20, 44, 129, 150. *See also* Weather
Wind Cave National Park, 108
Wolves, 102, 159
Wounded Knee, Battle of (1890), 164
Wright, Frank Lloyd, quoted, 27

Y

Yarrow *(Achillea millefolia)*, *151*
Yucca, 27

Z

Zolite crystals, 53